HOOKED ON TROUT

HOOKED ON TROUT

**How and where
to catch large trout
in New Zealand**

RON GILES

REED

Published by Reed Books, a division of Reed Publishing (NZ) Ltd, 39 Rawene Rd, Birkenhead, Auckland. Associated companies, branches and representatives throughout the world.

ISBN 0 7900 0742 8

© 2000 Ron Giles

The author asserts his moral rights in the work.

Designed by Sunny H. Yang
Typeset by Sharon Whitaker
Front cover photographs and pages 11 and 103 by David Hallett
Maps by Jonette Surridge

First published 2000

Printed in New Zealand

Established in 1907, Reed Publishing (NZ) Ltd
is New Zealand's largest book publisher, with over 300 titles in print.

For details on all these books visit our website:
www.reed.co.nz

# Acknowledgements

Thanks are due to the following people:

To Steve Wright whose pragmatism turned a vague idea into a reality;

To Steve's contact at Reed, Publishing Manager Peter Janssen, who came up with the structure that made the book a viable proposition;

To Jo Elliott, my editor, for her unfailing enthusiasm and patience with a tyro author;

To map illustrator Jonette Surridge for the clarity her maps give to my text;

To all my regular fishing companions over the years — Austin; Pete; Walter; Frank and Robbie; Speeds, Stevo & Riggers — your contributions to the book are obvious;

To Rory, fishing companion extraordinaire. I am very lucky to have found such a perfect fishing mate;

To my photographer — Glenn Martin, with ideas from my brother-in-law, Tony — your skills enhanced the book considerably;

To designer Sunny for her work with the photographs;

To our holiday companions Helen and Paul for allowing themselves to be steered into destinations with a distinctly 'fishy' nature;

To my family for all their help and encouragement — Nev for the company on many a fishing excursion and for 'minding the shop' while Dad was incommunicado up some river, and Tanya for all her hard work in editing and proofreading. A tighter, tidier work was the result.

But most of all, thanks to Sue for all her encouragement even when it resulted in many lonely nights while I was away fishing — again. Her attitude of 'if you can't stop him — join him' saw her develop a love for the New Zealand wilderness as we tramped up many of the rivers in this book.

Contents

Introduction

I must confess to being a fairly ordinary trout fisherman. The only reason I have caught a lot of fish — and a few big fish — is that I put most of my effort into discovering where they are to be found. If you are an expert fly-fisher and have fished extensively around New Zealand, this book is probably not for you. You will already know many of the waters I describe and how to fish them. But if you have mainly fished just your local waters, or the famous river down the road, and are looking for more challenges, read on.

The idea for the book came from talking to many trout-fishing people throughout the country, as well as to tackle-shop staff. The overwhelming consensus was that there was a demand for a book that concentrated on some of the excellent but less well-known trout-fishing waters of New Zealand. There are many books on fishing the famous waters, such as Lake Taupo or the Tongariro, Buller or Mataura rivers, and a guide to all the trout-fishing waters of New Zealand already exists in the form of John Kent's thorough series. But what trout-fishers seemed to be looking for was a book that told them where to go to catch either a big fish or a lot of fish, and also told them which technique was most likely to bring success on that particular water.

The lack of such guidance appeared to be confirmed by my own fruitless efforts to find out which rivers would yield the quality of fishing I was seeking. This included information on such matters as scenery, an area's relative isolation and how heavily fished a stretch of water was. When I read all the available literature, I did not gain much specific information. Numerous magazine articles would cover the superb fishing available when the big runs went through the Tongariro, or relate how a writer caught a 10-pounder in Rocky Creek No. 5 somewhere on the West Coast.

But only the odd book gave details of good fishing waters beyond the famous few, and these tended not to give too many clues about where exactly to fish or which specific techniques to use. *Hooked on Trout* is an attempt to fill this perceived gap in the trout-fishing book market. Of course, there is no guarantee that the entire fish population of a river described in the following pages has not been washed away in a horrendous flood since the book was written — but that's trout-fishing.

Be warned: many of the waters I write about can be reached only by a long drive or walk — in a few cases, both! The one thing I have noticed in recent years is that the popular waters are getting a real thrashing. Anyone who has recently fished in the Taupo or Nelson regions will probably agree. It is increasingly hard to catch good trout in these heavily fished areas, so I have spent a lot of time looking for waters further afield and then fishing them. Hopefully the reader will benefit from this research.

I remember reading a book review that criticised the author for including too many 'I' stories. It was the reviewer's opinion that expert anglers cannot be bothered reading about how someone caught the 'big one'. Accordingly, I have included such stories only to illustrate the quality of the fish in a particular water. I have also kept them fairly brief, so the reader can easily skip forward to where details of the technique used are given. Most of the techniques described are not original. I have gleaned them either from the wide variety of trout-fishing books I have studied or from the verbal accounts of anglers much better than me of how they overcame a particular problem. Similarly, the fly patterns given are not necessarily original but are those that have worked well on the waters described. Often a pattern features a modification that made it easier for me to tie or that I found made it more attractive to fish.

I hope the following chapters help you find some real quality fishing, and that even if the fish are not biting, you appreciate the beauty of the place in which you find yourself. Meanwhile I'll be out there researching the next lot of good spots.

Tight lines!

Ron Giles

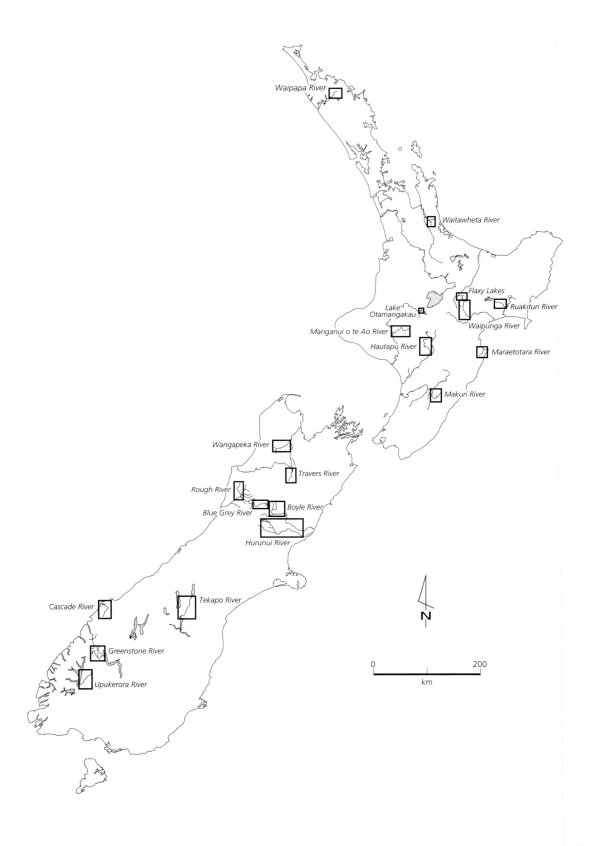

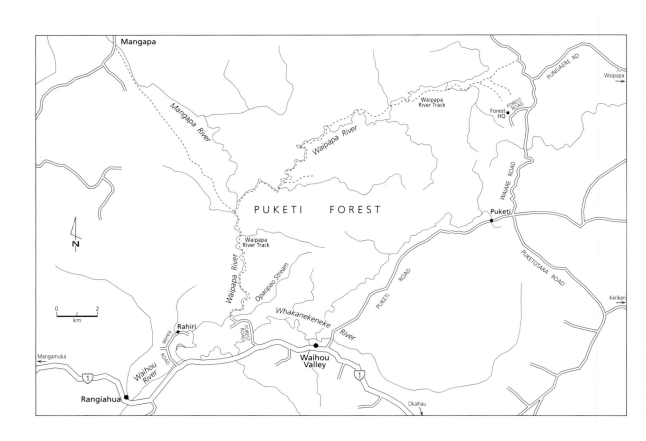

Waipapa River
Tactics for midsummer fishing

DESCRIPTION AND DIRECTIONS

The scenic Waipapa River rises in the northeast corner of the beautiful Puketi Forest in central Northland. For the greater part of its length, it wends its way through the 8061 ha forest, venturing beyond it only for the last few kilometres. The shade provided by the mature kauri forest ensures the river is cool, making it one of the few rivers in Northland able to sustain a trout population.

The upper reaches are accessible by way of the Waipapa River Track, which follows the river for most of its length. The track starts at the Puketi Forest Headquarters, off Waiare Road. It is about an hour's walk to the upper Waipapa. The river is small at this stage, the trout likewise. The upper reaches should be regarded more as a tramping excursion on which a rod can be taken for a flick along the way.

It is a two-day tramp from the forest headquarters to the end of the track. This walk takes you through some of the most beautiful native bush in Northland, the equal of the more famous Waipoua Forest, just up the road. Puketi Forest contains the Takapau kauri, the fourth largest kauri in New Zealand.

The river track emerges in the southwest corner of the park, accessed by Forest Road, off SH 1, north of Okaihau. Here the river is of medium size, with a classic pool–rapid–pool configuration. Rainbow trout average around 0.75 kg, but fish up to 2 kg can be found early and late in the season.

The track in the lower section is wide and flat, suggesting it was formed for dragging out large kauri. The river is wadeable in low summer flows, and even when it is high, it is quite easy to regain the track and walk up to the next pool. The bottom is usually very clean, the result of regular floods that also have the unfortunate effect of washing away much of the nymph life. This in turn means that after spawning, the trout tend to fall back to the lower reaches to find the food needed to build up condition for the next year's run.

Below the picnic area at the end of Forest Road, the river is slow and silty. During normal flows, it is not possible to wade across the river along this 1 km stretch. To fish further downstream, it is necessary to drive a kilometre to Rahiri, via Rahiri Settlement Road. This ends at the river by an attractive stretch of runs and riffles. From here it is possible to fish a couple of kilometres upstream, as far as the start of the slow stretch, or to go downstream to an interesting series of pools, which extends as far as the junction with the Whakanekeneke River.

The Whakanekeneke is easily discoloured by rain, being a slower river than the Waipapa and flowing mainly through farmland. It is also slow to clear, making the lower reaches of the Waipapa, below where the rivers merge, not particularly pleasant to fish. Flowing as it does into the very tidal Waihou River, the lower Waipapa clears noticeably quicker when the tide is on the way out.

A benefit of the lower Waipapa's tidal nature is the runs of whitebait that occur, and the larger trout that follow them upstream. If you fish the lower stretches during the whitebait season you will have a good chance of picking up a 3–4 kg fish. But the farmland setting is not as idyllic as the native forest higher up. It is therefore necessary to decide which is more important — the size of the fish or the beauty of the surroundings. Certainly, any lack of big fish along the upper reaches is more than compensated for by the unique experience of fishing in magnificent kauri forest.

TALES AND TECHNIQUES

The Waipapa River will never be famous for the size of its trout nor the intensity of its spawning runs, but it is unique in that it flows through a primeval kauri forest. When fishing the Waipapa, it is hard not to feel remorse for the actions of our forebears. It is difficult to understand how they could have cut down so many giant trees. They may not have realised the larger kauri were over 2000 years old, but surely they could have worked out it was going to take an awfully long time to replace them.

To my mind, felling a forest giant is similar to killing a large trout for a trophy: how many years will it take for another fish to grow to the same size? Hopefully we are starting to take note of the ecological impact of our actions — walking through the remnants of a once-great forest tends to make us more aware of the consequences. As Professor J.T. Salmon points out, of an estimated 1.2 million ha of original kauri forest, only a few hundred hectares remain pristine. Fishing a river that winds its way through some of these remnants is a pleasant way of being reminded to think about what we are leaving for future generations.

The fishing in the Waipapa can be patchy. On some visits you wonder if there are any decent fish in the river. Local residents blame such scarcity on the use of 1080 poison to kill possums, which threaten the forest's population of kokako. That there were significant numbers of this rare native bird in the forest was only realised in 1979. The discovery forced the end of kauri logging, which had continued up until then. The Department of Conservation (DoC) makes regular aerial drops of poisoned carrots, and local residents claim that after each drop, dead trout are to be found floating down the river. They say a good proportion of these are in the 1–2 kg bracket. However, my own discussions with a DoC birdlife officer cast some doubt on this theory. He was adamant that 1080 poison quickly breaks down into harmless by-products when it comes into contact with water.

As it happened, my last visit to the Waipapa was a few days after a poison drop, and the fishing did seem to have fallen off compared with previous excursions to the same area. I suppose I could have blamed the DoC programme, although the temporary lack of fish was more than compensated for by the beauty of the river.

In fact, it is hard to concentrate on fishing when you are wading up one of the most scenic rivers in the North Island. Nikau, ponga, fern and rimu line the riverbank, with the occasional kauri or totara towering above. Fantails flutter about in a nearby tree, distracting you from the drift of the fly. Fortunately, most of the trout in the forest section of the river are juveniles that take with a savage rush and tend to hook themselves without any assistance. They do, however, give a good account of themselves as they then race downstream. The banks along the lower bush reaches are mainly shingle, and this makes landing a fish relatively easy: it is usually not long before you can bulldoze it onto the gravel and free the fly.

In normal flows, the fish lie in the eye of a pool, as you would expect. Casting up to the rapids at the head of the pool and allowing the nymph to tumble over the ledge is usually the most productive tactic. The fish do not appear to like the slower midsections of the larger pools, as these tend to be rather silted up. It is likely that any insect life there is regularly washed away by floods and that the fish rely on food being brought down the river.

When the river is low, as is often the case during the droughts of a northern summer, different tactics are required. It is necessary to give some thought to where trout are likely to lie as the water temperature rises. Even though the forest shades much of the river, the summer sun still warms the open stretches, and the trout seek the cooler or more oxygenated water. A major source of cooler water is an incoming stream, so trout tend to congregate where streams join the main river.

The preference of trout for such cool spots is graphically illustrated by a story told to me by Rory, my fishing mate from Hawke's Bay. Rory and a friend were trekking down a tributary of the Esk River one summer's day. They had risen early, and it was still only semi-light when they arrived at the main river. They could not believe their eyes as they stared into the pool where the small stream entered the Esk. Dozens of brown trout were clustered in the flow of cool water. As they watched, the sun came up and the trout started to slink off into the depths and under rocky ledges.

The stream entered the river in its middle section, where it was exceptional to spot more than a couple of trout in a day's fishing. Rory believed the brown trout he saw that day sought cover during the day and fed only at night. Certainly the Esk River gets extremely low — and warm — during the usual Hawke's Bay summer drought. The stream, as well as providing cool, oxygenated water, would have been a good source of food. Flowing out of a bush region it would have been carrying drowned insects, such as terrestrials, thus proving an attractive place for trout to 'hang out'.

There are numerous small inflows of water along the Waipapa. Many are not big enough to deserve the title of stream or creek — a more apt term is rivulet — but they are cool and carry plenty of food. A useful trick is to walk along the track until you reach a rivulet, then follow this through the bush to where it trickles into the river. The inflow is likely to be obscured by foliage and not obvious to the eye when fishing up the river. Mark the spot and make your way to where you can cross the river and fish up to the trout that are hopefully feeding below the cool inflow.

Cool spots are also found in riffles — stretches of medium-paced water flowing over rocks close enough to the surface to give it a ruffled appearance. A riffle is distinguished from a rapid, where the water is fast-flowing or the rocks are exposed, and a run, where the rocks are deeper and the surface therefore disturbed only a little or not at all.

Trout love riffles for the cover they provide and the food that is carried past their noses. They are able to rest where the shelter of the rocks on the bottom provides quiet water in the middle of the river. From here they can see any morsel drifting down the centre of the river and intercept it with

minimum effort. While doing so, they are protected by the ruffled water above, as predators cannot easily see into the river because the light is being refracted.

A good looking riffle on the Waipapa.

Trout generally feed in pools in low-light conditions and move up into the riffles during the day. This is especially so in the heat of summer, when pools become too warm. At this time of year, it can be quite surprising where fish are found in the middle of the day. Even swift-flowing rapids can yield fish if the water is deep enough to give them sufficient cover. The reduced flow of summer enables the trout to stay in water that would normally be too fast to occupy. Rapids and riffles are also cooler than pools, as the turbulence means the sun's impact is reduced. Turbulence also oxygenates the water, which is critical to trout survival. Anyone who has seen semicomatose trout in warm, still pools in March will testify to this. It is generally considered that 20ºC is the highest water temperature trout can safely tolerate — which is why the warmer waters of the North are, generally, not a suitable environment for them.

As the middle section of the Waipapa does not have many riffles, it is essential to fish any you find very thoroughly. Trout tend to congregate there, leaving the pools barren. This lesson was first brought home to me after a day on the Whirinaki River in mid-February many years ago. Not knowing the river, I had been fishing the delightful pools in the middle reaches around Minginui. I had fished carefully but failed to raise a trout all day. It was very frustrating, as the water looked good and I knew the river had a substantial trout population.

That night, I read a book that included some observations about fishing the Whirinaki. The author described how he and his friends had been camped at the riverside, enjoying an 'after-match' bevy as the sun went down. Discussion turned to how they had given the good-looking pools a real going-over but with a distinct lack of success. All of a sudden, the riffle in front of them came alive with feeding trout. They could not believe this shallow, nondescript-looking stretch of water could hold so many fish. Being smart lads, they concentrated exclusively on fishing the riffles the next day. The results were amazing, with large numbers of fish being caught.

I absorbed this information and the following morning was back in the same area but ignored the pools completely. I did not have quite the same success as those guys, but I did manage to connect with a few fish, including a satisfying 2.5 kg brown — from the top of a shallow riffle.

Barren pool.

One summer, when the river was very low, I looked closely into the pools on the Whirinaki and found they were rather barren. There was the odd rock but otherwise they had plain, sandy bottoms.

When you think about this, it becomes obvious there is nowhere for nymph life to exist in such a barren environment. Nymphs need the cover and protection of rocks to survive: they would soon be swept from a featureless pool. That is why the Whirinaki nymphs were to be found clinging to the rocks in the riffles. Where the food was, the trout were too. On the Waipapa River, the big, slow pools are similarly fishless during the heat of the day, the trout having found food and shelter in the riffles.

Another spot in which trout are likely to be found in summer is where foliage overhangs the river's edge, particularly where there is an indentation in the bank, creating a recess with slower water. The foliage provides shade as well as cover, while the main flow of the river is only a few centimetres away and any food floating past can be easily intercepted. A trout generally feels safe only if it has cover overhead, and this is usually provided by depth. However, in shallow summer flows, overhanging foliage or broken surface water provides an acceptable alternative to the safety of a deep pool. Summer fishing is a matter of working out where trout lie to avoid the high temperatures. If you can programme your mind to think like an overheated fish seeking cool water, the likely spots become more obvious and the fishing more productive.

This approach worked well for me one hot January day when I had grown tired of the beach and sought the coolness of the kauri forest. The river was low and the summer sun was pouring down, and it was a relief to escape into the shade of the trees. I wandered up the track, peering along each pool for signs of a stream entering the river. About a kilometre up from the picnic area I saw a bubbly creek about a metre wide tumbling a couple of metres down a fern-covered bank into the head of a pool. Picking my way through the sparse undergrowth, I slipped into the water a few metres down from the creek.

I had on a dull-coloured WF5F line with a 4 m leader tapering to 2 kg. This was coated with a sinking concoction (I still prefer the old-fashioned mixture of Fuller's Earth and detergent). A small yarn indicator was attached to the tippet junction. On went a size 14 beadhead Caddis and I was ready for business.

Thanks to the lack of wind, the first cast was a good one and the indicator bobbled down the feed line just below the stream mouth. It hesitated briefly and I lifted the rod. A strong fish raced down the pool and a

Fishing an incoming stream.

good battle ensued. Eventually a 1.75 kg jack rainbow lay in the shallows. He was released to ponder the mistake he had made and I re-entered the pool. A couple of casts later, another rainbow made the same mistake and was duly landed.

In all, the morning produced four nice fish — a satisfactory result on this river. Success was due to the time spent locating the most likely lies of the trout on such a hot day, and the use of light tackle in the low water. In the Far North, such low-water tactics are appropriate for most of summer.

Even though the beautiful Waipapa may be far from your favourite fishing rivers, its cool, bush-clad waters give you a chance to hone your fly-fishing skills while the rest of the family enjoy the beach just a few kilometres away.

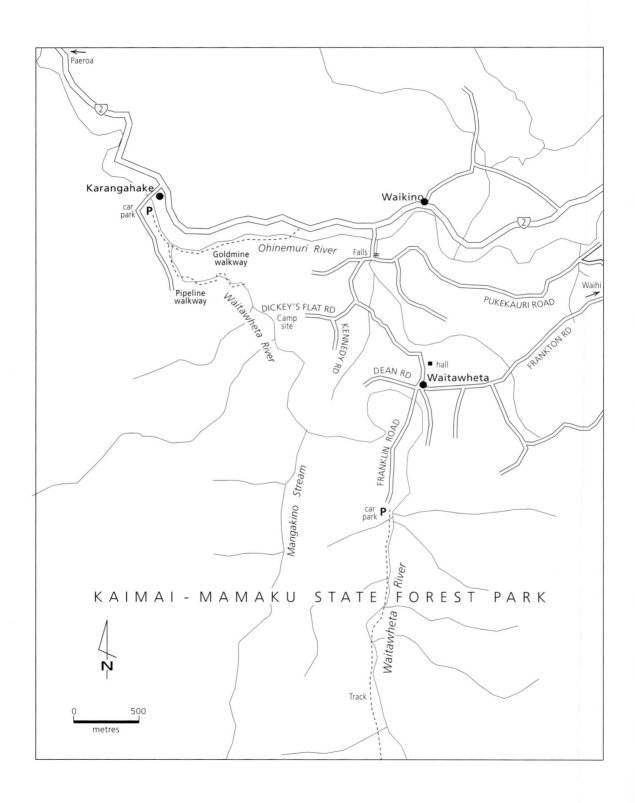

Paeroa

②

Karangahake ●
car
park P

Goldmine
walkway

Ohinemuri River Falls

Waikino ●

②

Pipeline
walkway

Waitaweheta River

DICKEY'S FLAT RD
Camp
site

KENNEDY RD

PUKEKAURI ROAD

Waihi →

FRANKTON RD

DEAN RD

■ hall

Waitawheta

Mangakino Stream

FRANKLIN ROAD

car
park P

KAIMAI - MAMAKU STATE FOREST PARK

Waitawheta River

N

0   500
metres

Track

Waitawheta River
The art of blind-nymphing

DESCRIPTION AND DIRECTIONS

The first encounter with this charming river is usually from the historic Goldmine Walkway, which starts from the first bridge over the Ohinemuri River at the beginning of the Karangahake Gorge. A few hundred metres along the track, the Waitawheta River flows into the Ohinemuri just opposite the site of an old stamping battery. From the junction, access up the Waitawheta Gorge is easy, as the track follows the water pipeline for the township of Paeroa.

The water in this section consists mainly of large, deep pools. It is necessary to clamber down from the track to fish a pool or two, before you are forced to regain the path. There is a lot of fishable water, but unless the trout are rising, a rather heavy style of fishing is required, as you have to get down to the deep-lying fish. However, it might be worth the effort, as fish up to 4 kg can be found in this section of the river.

After a few kilometres, the pipeline heads up a hill, and the access up the river is hard from the end of the pipeline track. It is easier to drive up to the next bridge and follow Waitawheta Road to Kennedy Road and then Dickey's Flat Road, which ends at a delightful campsite. This is very popular over summer, and the area receives a lot of angling pressure at that time of year. There is easy access up and down the river with a well-trodden path following it.

The water below the campsite is slow, with a rather featureless papa bottom, and it pays to walk well downstream to get to more interesting water. Above the campsite, it is possible to fish all the way up to the next access at Dean Road. Otherwise this stretch can only be accessed by asking permission from the farmers whose properties border the river. This is excellent water and holds more fish as it is not subject to the same amount of angling pressure. Both browns and rainbows are present, with an average weight of 1.2 kg and plenty of bigger fish up to 2.5 kg. This is pleasant fishing, with clear banks on the farmland side and attractive native bush on the far bank.

Near Waitawheta, Franklin Road crosses the river. There is reasonable fishing for several kilometres, as the river winds through farmland up to the end of Franklin Road, which is the start of the DoC track to the Waitawheta Forest Park. From here up, for the first 2 km, the river runs through farmland, and there are some productive deep, slow pools. The grassy banks afford easy access, but a low profile is necessary as there is some angling pressure on this stretch of water. There is a substantial population of browns, and in summer they often lie in the riffles between the pools.

After a couple of kilometres, a wide old logging track enters the native bush. In low summer flows, it is possible to wade up the river from here. In the higher flows of spring and late autumn, wading is impossible and it is necessary to push through the bush to access each pool. With a bit of effort, most pools can be accessed from the track, and the fishing is good early or late season. Again, browns and rainbows of up to 2 kg are to be found in the short deep pools and will readily take a small beadhead Hare'n'Copper or a size 12–14 Pheasant Tail.

It is possible to fish for many kilometres up the river, but the trout tend to be smaller and less numerous up towards the headwaters. When the flow is really low, most of the fish drop back down the river. However, the enchanting native bush and the company of fantails may more than compensate for a lack of fish.

TALES AND TECHNIQUES

The Waitawheta is a real gem. It varies from a small stream running through lovely natural bush, to slow, stretches meandering through farmland, to big pools in a boulder-filled gorge. The river holds a good head of fish, with an average weight of 1.5 kg. A drift/dive survey in the summer of 1997–98 found a level of 60 fish/km, with a suprisingly high number of large trout — 'large' meaning over 40 cm (16 inches) long.

The larger fish were believed to have moved up from the Ohinemuri River, seeking the cooler waters of the Waitawheta — cooler because of that river's bush-shaded upper reaches. The more open Ohinemuri, with its slower water and shallow stretches, tends to warm up considerably in summer (as the number of kids who swim in the bigger pools in the heat of summer presumably testifies).

But the Ohinemuri also has a big reputation with those that fish it. The flow is not fast and is broken by many rocks and boulders. This makes it

The upper Waitawheta.

pleasant to fish as you pitch your fly in the slower run behind a slab-sided boulder. It holds a surprising number of fish, considering its easy access and the high number of anglers it attracts.

The gorge section of the Waitawheta, just up from the junction, is likely to hold many of the Ohinemuri fish tired of the huge fluctuations in the level of that flood-prone river. However, the heavier gear needed to take them is not as much fun as the lightweight tackle required further up the river. There, especially in midsummer, it is necessary to use a 4- or 5-weight rod and to be very stealthy in your approach.

I learned this rather belatedly when I was fishing the river one day in mid-March. The river was as low as I had ever seen it, as there had been no rain for two months. Arriving at the end of Franklin Road, I tackled up the 5-weight rod, putting on my favourite 'stealth-grey' fly line. Walking up the track, I decided to have a look in the first big pool, where the track starts to climb above the river. The shallow tail afforded an easy crossing, and I noted how slippery the rocks were; confirmation there had been no 'fresh' down the river for some time.

I ambled along the shingle bank, exercising little caution as the long, slow pool didn't look very 'fishy'. But as I peered into the clear water, six trout peered back at me. They all immediately swam down the pool to get away from the strange apparition on the bank, but the water was not really deep enough for them to hide anywhere, so they kept racing up and down the pool, probably figuring not much harm could come to them while they were moving. Short of my trying a Tongariro Hydro Pool foul-hooking job, there was no way these fish would be taking a fly for some time. I regained the track, suitably chastened by my lack of care.

As I looked up the river, I could see the next few hundred metres consisted of shallow flows of water broken up by the many rocks of that wide stretch. It was obvious that the water above could not shelter trout, and the only cover for some way upstream was the pool where I had just spooked the six fish. Oh well, they would still be there on the way back.

You have to be thick not to learn from such a dramatic experience, so the pool at the top of the long stretch of shallow rapids was about to be approached with a lot of care. I sidled into the tail very slowly to ensure I sent no waves up the slow pool. It is surprising in low flows how far a ripple from a wading angler will travel against the gentle current. I hunkered down, with my head below the edge of the scrub, and studied the far depths of the pool. As I had hoped, there were two shadows hard up against the rock face about 2.5 m deep, at the end of the tongue of the entry current.

It took a couple of casts to get the drift so the fly was swimming down the feed line near the far rock face. The first correct drift saw a positive response, and the small yarn indicator dipped satisfyingly. I lifted the rod and battle ensued. Not long after, a 1.5 kg rainbow was beached and the size 14 Green Caddis tail fly removed from its jaw. At least I had learned from my earlier mistake.

Further up the river, the pools became shallower and it was easy to see the bottom of even the deepest pool. I had my doubts whether any respectable trout would be happy to hang out in such unsafe places so I concentrated on the deeper riffles, where there was at least a little cover, plus the benefit of oxygenated water.

I could not spot anything in the riffle above the pool I'd just fished but the water looked deep enough to chance a flick. I had changed to a size 14

Pheasant Tail, and the copper in the traditional 'Sawyer' pattern was enough to sink it quickly in the gently flowing ripples. As the fly was sidling round a large rock, there was a sharp take and a feisty 1.2 kg brown shot upstream. With no current to aid its fight, it was quickly beached and released.

That was the end of the fish for the day. Despite a long walk up the track, stopping to look at the occasional pool, I saw no more trout. It was getting late, so I turned back, intending to give that first trout-filled pool a good going-over on the way. Reaching the bank above the pool, I crept through the bracken to look down into the pool . . . only to see a fisherman slowly retrieving line as his fly drifted through the deep pool. I stared hard into the water from my elevated vantage point, but even through my Polaroids could see nothing. The fish, after all the attention they had received, had obviously found a hidey-hole somewhere and disappeared from sight. I didn't feel like ruining the solitary angler's expectations, so quietly backed away and continued on to the car. I'd had a lovely walk through some beautiful bush on a gorgeous sunny day, and my couple of trout I considered a bonus.

Most of my best results on the Waitawheta have come from the middle section, where the river does the big loop between the Kennedy Road and Dean Road access points (the latter is spelt 'Deam' on the signpost). The first time I fished the river, I stayed at the Auckland Freshwater Anglers' Hut on a farm in this area. It was early December, and I had the best part of the day before I was due at the Kaueranga River to pick up my son from a camp.

At that time of the year the flows in this stretch are strong, and the fish cannot easily be seen in the deep, shaded pools or the numerous rocky riffles. For the proficient blind-nympher, this is ideal water. Some fly-fishers steadfastly maintain blind-nymphing is for beginners or for anglers who cannot catch 'sighted' fish. This is to ignore the fact that in many stretches of water, in many rivers, you may never be able to spot fish. They may be lying deep in the pools, or in the rapids at the head of a pool, or they may be rendered invisible by peat-stained water. It is also to ignore the range of skills to be accumulated from practising this particular technique.

Blind-nymphing is a state of mind. It is absorbing and demands intense concentration, but that is the attraction. You certainly don't think of work problems or the unmown lawn when you are blind-nymphing. If your mind does wander from the task in hand, you can guarantee that is when a fish will take and your reaction will probably be too slow. You need to be concentrating on the drift of the line, watching for a telling movement of the indicator. You have to be hyperalert and attuned to the many nuances of the river's behaviour — its currents, eddies, swirls, pockets and laminar flows. There is no active thought process, just an automatic response — to mend, to adjust, to watch, to strike when something is not quite right with the drift of the line.

After you have hooked a fish, you will replay the sequence of events in your mind in an effort to identify what caused you to strike when you did. Usually you will be unable to isolate the trigger for your action. It will have been an instinctive reaction based on years of watching a natural drift of the leader. When there is any small change to the anticipated drift, your arm lifts up before you have consciously thought why you are striking. Frank Sawyer, in his book *Nymphs and the Trout*, describes this very aptly: 'You see nothing, feel nothing, yet something prompts you to lift the rod tip, some little whisper in your brain to tell you a fish is at the other end of your line.' This is particularly so when you have been fishing for a few days and your responses have become finely honed and entirely automatic.

This is the Zen state of blind-nymphing, the joy of it and the addiction to it. Sure, hooking a visible fish is the most satisfying achievement in fly-fishing, but blind-nymphing is an art form of its own, with its own place among fly-fishing techniques. To successfully fish a variety of waters proficiency in blind-nymphing is essential.

Probably the most important blind-nymphing technique is dead-drifting — matching the natural flow of the current in which your fly is drifting. Too fast or too slow a drift and your nymph will interest only a small or stupid fish. It is rare to catch a sizeable fish on a bad, draggy drift. When you are fishing a stretch of water with complicated currents, it may take you several drifts through the pool to get the correct series of line mends and adjustments to see the fly drifting naturally. You will know instinctively when you achieve that perfectly dead drift, and will automatically be in an alert state, ready for the strike.

A bad drift means you can relax, as you know nothing much will be tempted by the unnatural path of the nymph. Of course, there may be times when you induce a take by adding movement to your fly, but this will depend on the type of fly and the nature of the water. If you are fishing a free-swimming Caddis, twitching the nymph will produce a natural pattern of movement. However, this will tend to be effective only in slow water, as in faster water a caddis is more likely to be at the mercy of the current than to move of its own accord. Similarly, some mayfly nymphs have a jerky movement and imparting some motion to the fly may help imitate the real thing.

Recently there has been some debate about the effectiveness of the technique of raising a beadhead nymph at the end of a drift. This is similar to the technique known as the 'Leisenring lift', in honour of its inventor, James Leisenring. Both techniques cause the nymph to rise from the riverbed, imitating the rise to the surface of an emerging nymph. On slow days, this can induce a take by a fish that has ignored a dead drift. However, I would always try dead-drifting first and then resort to other 'move-the-fly' tactics if the trout prove to be rather uninterested. This is more likely be the case in the heat of the day, or when water temperatures are up and the trout seem semicomatose. That is the time to work on your induced-take techniques, but when the trout are active, you risk scaring a feeding fish with an unnatural movement of the nymph.

The middle stretches of the Waitawheta are ideal for a day's blind-nymphing, concentrating solely on the tip of the line. The fish in this section tend to be a bit larger than further up the river, and on that first day, I was impressed when a 2.5 kg brown intercepted my Hare'n'Copper Flashback as it tumbled down a riffle. The early-season fish was in good condition, so it may well have spent the winter in the Waitawheta rather than battling the Ohinemuri floods. She certainly gave a good account of herself, nosing into all the potential trouble spots on the far bank, seeking out some projection on which to leave the fly. It was necessary to wade out into the riffle on several occasions to ease her away from overhanging foliage and sharp obtrusions. Finally she was beached, and her distinctive dark spots stood out against her sun-kissed, silvery flank.

It is amazing just how much the colours of brown trout vary from fish to fish and from river to river. The browns that have those distinctive vivid spots make a canvas all of their own. As usual, I regretted not having brought my camera so I could capture the colours forever. Often, however, a photo cannot do justice to their beauty. I tried to store away the image for playback sometime when I was stuck in the office wishing I was on the river — which is most of the time.

The rest of the day saw two 1.5 kg rainbows come to the net before it was time to reluctantly retrace my steps. Neither trout had been spotted, and both had fallen to a nymph dead-drifted through a pool. It pays to put in a lot of work to perfect a dead drift, no matter what river you fish, as it is perhaps the most productive technique in New Zealand. The Waitawheta, with its plentiful supply of trout, is an ideal river on which to practise blind-nymphing. Its other attributes — the stunning scenery and a real sense of isolation — are bonuses.

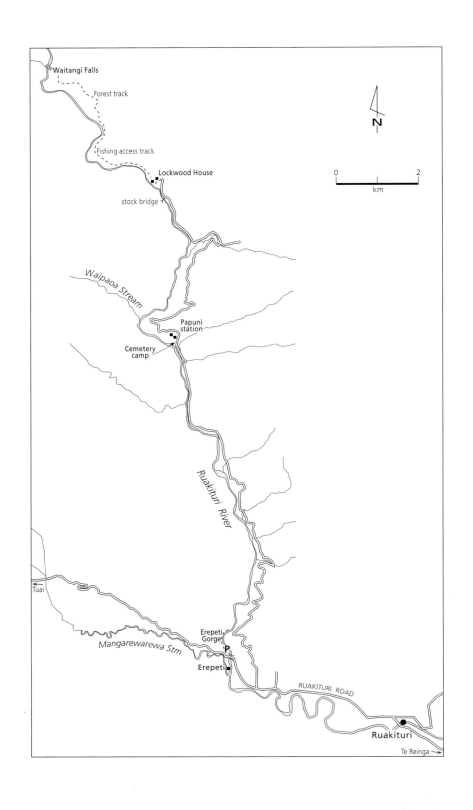

Waitangi Falls

Forest track

Fishing access track

Lockwood House

stock bridge

Waipaoa Stream

Papuni station

Cemetery camp

Ruakituri River

Tuai

Mangarewarewa Stm

Erepeti Gorge

P

Erepeti

RUAKITURI ROAD

N

0   2
km

Ruakituri

Te Reinga →

Ruakituri River
Riffle-fishing techniques

DESCRIPTION AND DIRECTIONS

The Ruakituri is an isolated river that rises in the remote Urewera National Park, draining the Huiarau Range and flowing through rugged bush before dropping 100 m over the Waitangi Falls. Above the falls, access is limited to those well-equipped trampers who are not only familiar with the terrain but also have sufficient experience to cope with rapid changes in weather conditions. Below the falls, the river tumbles down terraces of bedrock between steep, bush-flanked valley walls, until fingers of farmland meet it at the top end of Papuni Station.

The station is along Papuni Road, which is reached by turning right off Ruakituri Road, just before the Erepeti Gorge. Whether the road through Papuni Station is public or private has been the subject of court action. At the time of writing, the road is open so long as you check in at Papuni Station homestead.

From the road end there is a track up to the Waitangi Falls, but to fish above the falls is too far for a day fisherman. Below the falls the river is strewn with colossal boulders, brought down by the regular flash floods the Ruakituri trout have to endure. There is a huge variety of water, ranging from strenuous rapids to deep, slow pools flanked by sentinel boulders, to riffly runs that just have to hold fish. It is no place for fine leaders and delicate techniques. Anything less than a 2.5 kg leader is pointless, as the strong Ruakituri trout make use of their angler-unfriendly environment. Browns and rainbows are found in equal proportion, dependent only on the type of water fished. The size of fish can be daunting. They average 2 kg, and there are plenty of 5 kg individuals in residence.

The gorge behind Papuni Station sees the main tributary, the Waipaoa Stream, enter the river. The stream does not appear substantial at the point of entry, but the impression is deceiving as it runs underground, thanks to a rockfall a kilometre upstream. It is well worth the slog up to the fishable water.

Below the junction, the river slows its headlong charge and there is more of the classic rapid-pool-rapid pattern common to most rivers. There are more fish, too, but they are smaller, with a lot of rainbows weighing around 1.5 kg. The whole stretch is easily accessed by getting permission from the farmhouses along Ruakituri Road.

You can get into Erepeti Gorge itself via a track that starts in the clearing on the right just over the Erepeti Bridge. This section of the river is characterised by huge, deep pools set among boulders the size of a house. The river has cut a deep channel through the papa rock, and the pools cannot be plumbed by a fly-fisher. There are some big fish in this section but seriously heavy tackle is required to get anywhere near them unless they are feeding on the surface.

Emerging from the long gorge, the river takes on a different character as it meanders through farmland to meet the Hangaroa River at Te Reinga. Access is easy through the farms bordering the river. Along this section there is a better chance of spotting fish, but great stealth is required as there is not much cover. The river has lost its impetus and flows wider and slower. There is more weed growth in summer, which can be annoying. Long leaders are essential, and the increased angling pressure in the more accessible lower reaches makes the trout rather wary.

The Ruakituri then meets the Hangaroa River and their combined flow crashes down the Te Reinga Falls and joins the Wairoa River at Frasertown.

TALES AND TECHNIQUES

Whatever type of water you prefer to fish, the Ruakituri can offer it. You can fish dry, nymph or wet. You can fish big slow pools, fast turbulent flows, pools of huge depth, rocky riffles, and swirly backwaters. You can fish in rugged Urewera bush, in deep, shadowed gorges, or from farmland meadows. Which river has more variety? Not to mention fish that commonly go over 5 kg? Whatever criteria you use, the river has something for everyone.

This was never more dramatically demonstrated than on my first visit. My Napier fishing mate, Rory, and I had decided to spend a week at the river. We stayed at Cemetery Camp, just down from Papuni Station. With the permission of the farmer, we had been fishing the stretches of water up from the end of the farm road. The track to the Waitangi Falls starts here, and most days we walked up it an hour or so before starting to fish.

There is some excellent water above where the track leaves the river.

The first stretch is a long, rock-strewn run, flanked by steep bush on one side and overgrown farmland on the other. At the top of the run is a beautiful pool that remains etched in my memory. The main flow of the river pours through a narrow chute, before spreading out into a wide pool dotted with huge boulders. In and around the big rocks are numerous secondary flows. These enable trout to shelter from the strong current while sampling the steady flow of food drifting past their snouts.

I went to fish this pool while Rory stayed around the slower pools further down. I had on a size 8 Stonefly with a size 14 Flash Harrey — basically a rough Hare'n'Copper with a pearl Flashabou wing-case. Choosing a secondary flow that came round a large boulder on my side of the river, I tossed up the rig with the usual open loop. This was to avoid getting a hook through an ear as the upstream wind lowered the back cast.

In plopped the two flies a metre above the boulder, and the heavily weighted Stonefly dragged its baby brother down very swiftly. They were carried around the boulder and then swung into the pocket behind. The indicator stopped abruptly, and I struck hard to straighten the leader in the turbulent currents. Nothing happened. Then the indicator slowly moved out into the main current — and kept going! The fish was big and strong and unruffled by this temporary distraction. On up towards the head of the pool it went. I gave it heaps of sidestrain. There was an impasse for about 30 seconds as it pulled against the powerful butt of the 6/7 rod. After an agonising time, the fish was turned and started coming back to my side of the river.

I was grateful I had decided to take the heavier rod with the more solid butt. You can break a lighter rod trying to bulldoze a fish of that size. After a few more turns around the pool for the trout, and a fair bit of clambering up and down boulders for me, the fish was beached between the rocks. A fabulously proportioned brown hen lay at my feet. I pulled out my camera and took a couple of shots, then marked her length against my rod butt. After extracting the fly, I steered her back into the flow and off she took, undamaged but no doubt a little wiser.

I sat down on a rock and measured her length using the mark on the rod. Thirty-one inches (78 cm)! I had caught a couple of 30-inch Mohaka rainbows that had weighed in at over 10 lb (4.5 kg), and this fish had been much deeper and wider than those. I decided 12 lb (5.5 kg) was a realistic estimate to claim, before she grew a couple more during the evening storytelling.

A 12 lb Ruakituri brown.

When I had regained my composure, I fished the rest of the pool for another 30 minutes but without success. It was likely the pool had been too disturbed by the big fish thrashing about, so I made my way back down the river. I fished fairly quickly along the way, as I did not want Rory fretting over my absence. I was also keen to tell him all about the 'big one'.

Rory was ensconced in his favourite pool just opposite where the track leaves the river. As I gingerly crossed the slippery tail of the rapids above, he waded out. As I drew closer he bent down and held out something. It was a stick.

'What's that? Your only catch today?' I enquired politely.

'It's my fish, smartass,' he replied.

'Doesn't look much like a fish to me. Are you sure you haven't been on the whisky already?'

'Yeah, yeah,' replied Rory. 'It's the size of the rainbow I caught right here one hour ago. Thirty-one inches and twelve pounds. So beat that!'

Well, it was my pleasure to inform him that although I could not beat his fish, I could certainly match it. We sat down and told each other the story of our big fish. It didn't take long to work out we had caught our 12-pounders at around the same time but 2 km apart. Unfortunately for Rory, he didn't have his camera with him so had to rely on his stick for evidence. Those who know the story now always ask him, 'Caught any good sticks lately?'

Rory with his 31-inch stick.

Rory had caught his fish in very different water from mine. The pool he loved was a big slow one, some 40 m long, with papa rock forming the far bank. The water moved very slowly past the edge of the papa bank, and you just knew it was deeply undercut. This made it a perfect place to harbour big trout, offering cover, depth and a ready flow of food. I had found it a bit slow and boring, but Rory, with his more patient approach, had struck the big time. He only had to cast at the top of the inflow before communing with nature as his fly made its leisurely way through the pool. You could even walk your fly down the pool and fish the entire stretch with just one cast.

When I had fished there a few days before, I had tended to lose concentration during the fly's painfully slow progress. This was fatal, as the takes in the slow water were very gentle. The indicator tended only to hesitate briefly, or to move almost imperceptibly sideways. Rory disliked casting heavy flies, so slow water that needed only light nymphs suited him fine. Such is the attraction of the Ruakituri — something for everyone.

Later on that trip, we decided to make the big effort to tramp to the Waitangi Falls and fish above them, in water that was known for big trout. We knew our fishing time would be limited, as it supposedly took three hours from the road end to the falls, with some rugged country on the way. For the first hour, the track followed the river, passing water we had fished in previous days. Then the well-formed track veered away and headed straight up a steep, heavily bushed ridge.

We laboured for another hour and reached a point where there was a boundary marker noting that we were now in a national park. Well, whoever administered the park in those days must have been short of cash, as the track petered out at that point. Even the usual orange metal markers nailed to trees were nowhere to be seen. We did see some strips of orange plastic tape stuck to branches, however, and decided to follow those. This was fine until we came to a large clearing that looked as if it had been dug up with a rotary cultivator. Rory informed me this was the work of wild pigs. It was hard to believe how they could root up so much earth with just their snouts.

On the far side of the clearing, we could see the magnificent Waitangi Falls framed by the dense bush, but they were still at least an hour away. We scouted round the edges of the clearing but there were no more plastic strips and no evidence of a track. We concluded we had been following markers left by hunters to guide them or their mates to pig-shooting heaven, and that there was no sense in carrying on. Getting lost in such wild country would be asking for trouble.

As we retraced our steps through the dense bush, I thought about how British soldiers a hundred years before must have had similar problems. A company of fully equipped infantry had chased the wily Maori chief Te

Kooti all the way from Gisborne through this only-just-penetrable jungle. Te Kooti had led his pursuers upstream, but whenever the army came to a gorge, they had to make their way out of the valley, over the steep ridge and back down again — all the while dragging artillery and carrying other heavy equipment. Needless to say, Te Kooti made short work of the weary remnants in a well-planned ambush not much further upstream.

We eventually regained the river and managed to pick up a fish each, but this was poor reward for six hours of effort. If you have only a day at your disposal, it is probably better to fish up the river below the falls rather than try to get above them.

The Erepeti Gorge offers a prospect different from that of the upper river. To fish its incredibly deep pools you have to get 'down'n'dirty', and casting heavy lead-weighted nymphs on 6 m leaders isn't everyone's idea of fun. A big fish may make it worthwhile, but it is easy to lose such fish in the gorge pools. They tend to go deep into the tumble of rocks at the head and just not come out, no matter what tricks you try. I don't particularly enjoy fishing the gorge, soon tiring of chucking the heavy flies around, especially if the wind is blowing.

It's a lot easier to wait until late afternoon or early evening, when the fish come out to feed nearer the surface. Rory and I decided to do this one day on our second trip to the Ruakituri, and wandered down to the long stretch of riffles below Cemetery Camp. I had read that fish moved up in early evening to feed in the riffles, and I wanted to try a new technique I thought might suit such water. I chose a good looking riffle, and Rory went further on to fish the next pool down.

The flow looked rather swift, and I was starting to doubt if a fish would bother making the effort required to hold in this broken water. As usual, the trout had other ideas, and on my second drift down the riffle the indicator disappeared. I struck hard — and snapped off the fly. An expletive disturbed the quiet of the evening. Tying on another offering, I recast.

I was using what is now called a 'short-lining' technique. I first read of its use in Charles Brooks' *Nymphing for Larger Trout*. Brooks used a sinking line and fished downstream with heavily weighted nymphs. Instead of a sinking line, however, I tried the technique using a floater. Following Brooks' method, you cast 45 ft (14 m) across and upstream. As the line comes down towards you, instead of retrieving with your line hand, you lift the rod to take in the excess line. (Because the water is so fast, you'd have difficulty manually retrieving line quickly enough to stay in touch with the fly.) As the fly passes you, you lower the rod to allow more line

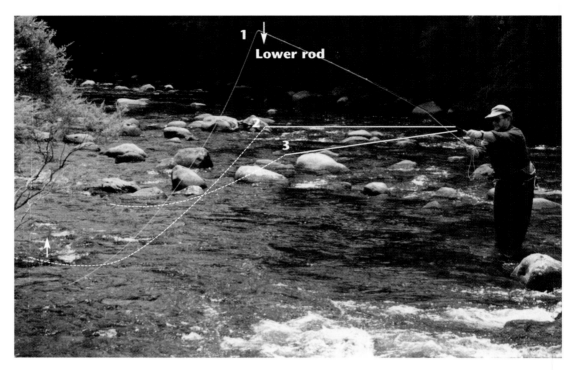

1
↓
Lower rod

2
3

Modified Brooks technique.

onto the water. This has the effect of lengthening the dead drift of the nymphs. You then fish out the drift, allowing the line to tighten at the end of the drift. This brings the nymphs off the bottom as though they were swimming to the surface. As the line tightens further, the nymphs continue to rise. Be ready for a heavy take if a fish sees them. By giving the line a twitch at this point, you can give the flies a bit more action.

With Brooks' sinking-line technique, it is normal to recover the flies with a varying retrieve. With a floating line, however, the nymphs are pulled up much nearer the surface and there is not much point in retrieving when they are high in the water. When the flies have risen, it is time to recast. Because you have heavy flies on, it is best not to false-cast. Lift the rod high and use the drag of the current to load it. Now pull firmly with your line hand to break the surface tension between the water and the line. As the line breaks free, swing the rod forward, pulling further down with your line hand to generate more kinetic energy. Using an open loop, chuck the whole rig 30 ft or so (about 10 m) across and up the river.

The aim of this modified Brooks technique is to get down quickly in the fast water but to use the rod to control the excess line. It is best used with big rough-water flies, and a Woolly Worm is always a good fly to start with.

It was a Woolly Worm I had snapped off on the strike. I tied on another, attached a new tail Flash Harrey and chucked them in at 45 degrees up the riffle. Nothing happened on that drift, so I moved down a pace or two. In they went again, and the indicator disappeared. This time I just lifted the rod and let the current hook the fish. Because fish do not have much time to inspect a fly in such fast water, they tend to hit hard. It is not necessary to strike strongly, as they virtually hook themselves. That's what happened with this fish, and off it went, careering down the riffle straight into the pool Rory was fishing. The abuse flowed soon after. The trout jumped high, landing with a splat that freed the hook. Derisive laughter from the far bank. Sometimes you wonder why you fish with such unsympathetic people. But at least the new technique had proven its worth.

It is a good one to try on faster water, and certainly suits the rough stretches of the Ruakituri. But it is only one of various techniques you will need to fish this river, as the variety of water and the size of the trout make it unique in New Zealand. Add to that the beauty of your surroundings and you have found trout-fishing heaven.

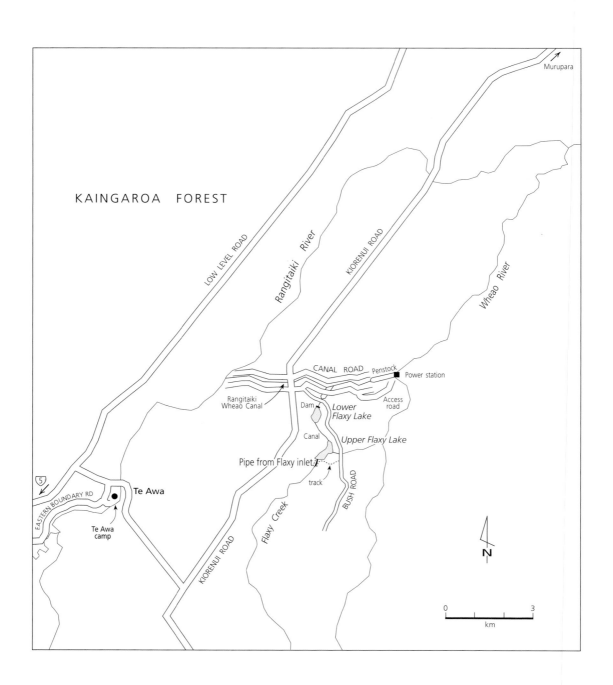

KAINGAROA FOREST

Murupara

LOW LEVEL ROAD

Rangitaiki River

KIORENUI ROAD

Wheao River

CANAL ROAD   Penstock ■ Power station

Rangitaiki
Wheao Canal

Dam   *Lower
Flaxy Lake*   Access
road

Canal   *Upper Flaxy Lake*

Pipe from Flaxy inlet

track   BUSH ROAD

5   Te Awa

EASTERN BOUNDARY RD

Te Awa
camp

KIORENUI ROAD

Flaxy Creek

N

0   3
km

Flaxy Lakes
Fishing for spawning trout

DESCRIPTION AND DIRECTIONS

The Flaxy Lakes, part of the Wheao Hydro Scheme, are found in the heart of the Kaingaroa Forest, reputedly the biggest man-made forest in the world. Access is from either the Rotorua–Murupara highway (SH 38) or the main Napier–Taupo highway (SH 5), but only if you have obtained a permit. This is easily obtained from the forest headquarters at Whaka-rewarewa. The permit is free, so don't even consider entering the forest without one, as security staff regularly patrol the area. When you get your permit, it pays to ask for a forest map at the same time, as it is very easy to get lost in the maze of tracks and roads, few of which are named and even fewer signposted.

It is about a 45-minute drive to the lakes from either entry point. Whichever way you come, it is necessary to get onto Kiorenui Road, which crosses the Rangitaiki/Wheao Canal. The waters diverted from the Rangitaiki River and the Flaxy Lakes feed this canal. The lakes were formed by damming the upper reaches of the Wheao River. Once known for the best dry fly-fishing in the entire North Island, this river was essentially ruined by the power scheme. There are a few kilometres of fishing available in the remains of the Wheao River below the power station, but the varying water level means it is not a stable trout environment and the fish there are not large.

The power scheme has, however, created some excellent fishing in both the Wheao Canal and the Flaxy Lakes. The canal isn't particularly scenic, but for those not bothered by relatively boring surroundings it offers productive fishing. The best time to fish is around dusk during summer, when you may get an exciting half-hour as the trout start rising. Unfortunately, use of the forest roads is allowed only during daylight hours, so you need to be camping in the forest to take advantage of this action. If this is not possible, it is a good plan to fish the Flaxy Lakes during the day and cruise along the canal on the way out, looking for signs of activity. Trout in the canal average 1.5 kg, with fish up to 3 kg being regularly caught.

The Flaxy Lakes are a couple of kilometres up Bush Road from the canal. There are two lakes, much the same size and linked by a narrow channel. There are a number of access tracks to different areas, although a 4WD may be required, especially after rain. To reach other parts of the lakes, it is useful to have some form of water transport, such as a float tube or a small rubber dinghy. Anything larger makes it more difficult to sneak up to the edges to fish the weed beds, where the better fish are to be found feeding.

At the top of the upper lake, the inlet water from Flaxy Creek enters through a large pipe, and it is through this that all the Flaxy trout must travel to spawn. This means that during the spawning season there is always some movement of fish from the lake, up the inlet channel and into the pipe. At other times, fish are to be found cruising the lake and normal lake-fishing techniques are successful. The Flaxy Lakes contain both brown and rainbow, the kind caught depending on the techniques used. The average weight is around 1.75 kg, but fish exceeding 4.5 kg are not uncommon.

TALES AND TECHNIQUES

The Flaxy Lakes are not known to many anglers, and to be honest I only discovered the quality of the fishing there by chance. The boys had decided the next expedition would be to the Horomanga River in the last week of the season, as the river was renowned for the large fish running up from Lake Aniwhenua to spawn. A keen team had been assembled to inflict significant damage on the local trout population. (Well, fleeting damage, as all would live to fight another day.) Joining me were Rory, my regular fishing mate, plus Frank and his son Robbie. We were all good mates from way back, and the trip looked like being the usual week of hard fishing days and convivial nights.

We booked in at Graeme and Joan Ryder's Aniwhenua Lodge for the last week of June, a time when the fish normally run up from the lake in good numbers. We had planned on hiring Graeme for one day to show us the river, as splitting the cost four ways made this a reasonable exercise. It had rained all the preceding week in the Rotorua area, so it looked as if conditions could be just right to strike a good run. We arrived at the lodge on the Monday afternoon and spent an enjoyable few hours fishing the lake from the banks. Several fish were landed, although they were mainly small, averaging around 1 kg.

The next day we rose, but not that early. We had intended to have a quiet night, partly in response to Frank's declaration that he had given up drinking beer as he was trying to lose weight. What transpired, though, was that although he didn't buy any beer he drank Robbie's. Naturally this soon ran out, as Robbie had not allowed for the extra consumption. Then it was time for Frank to broach the wine that was supposed to have been his only tipple. Really, though, it was probably the Scotch or three we had after dinner that did the damage.

A 9 lb brown from the Flaxy Lakes.

Rory was feeling very virtuous as he had gone to bed early, but all that meant was he was able to listen to the rain on the roof for longer. We gathered over breakfast to consider our options. Graeme popped in to say he had been down to check the river and it was dirtying up already, having not really recovered from the previous week's downpour. He said the Whirinaki was worse, so our only options were the Wheao Canal, the Wheao River below the powerhouse or the Flaxy Lakes. Rory and I looked at each other with a wry smile, as on two prior occasions we had tried to find the lakes without success. The fact that Rory would be a strong contender for the 'World's Worst Navigator' had not helped our efforts.

When we expressed our reservations, Graeme drew a quick sketch map to show us where we had gone wrong. He advised us to fish the inlet channel in the top lake, as the heavy rain should have prompted a few fish to run up to spawn in Flaxy Creek.

Fortunately, I had taken the precaution of getting a forest access permit before the trip. This meant we could load up the car and head straight for the lakes. As we left the lodge, the rain started to ease and our spirits lifted somewhat. We set off for Murupara and were soon able to confirm that the Horomanga was now very dirty and would be doubtful for fishing, even the next day. Arriving at Murupara, we turned onto the track that would take us to Kiorenui Road. It is about 40 minutes' drive from Murupara to the Wheao Canal. Following Graeme's detailed instructions, we turned left over the canal and took the first decent-looking road on the right. No wonder Rory and I had never found it before. There was no sign to indicate it was anything more than just another forest track, of which there are thousands in the Kaingaroa.

After a kilometre or so, the dam and the narrow part of the lake that fed water to the power station came into view. After 100 m of exit canal, the main lake lay before us. Rory was all excited, as he loves fishing lakes and this looked pretty good. It was beautifully still, with the surrounding low hills reflected in the tranquil water.

We carried on and found the narrow channel that linked the two lakes, the banks falling 10 m sheer to the water's edge. (Technically, the lakes are only one body of water, which most maps label just Flaxy Lake. However, because of the distinct separation of the two areas of water, locals refer to them as the Flaxy Lakes, so I have too.) We continued to follow Graeme's instructions and soon found a rough track through the pines. A few sharp turns later and we pulled up at the top end of the upper lake.

'Wow!' exclaimed Rory. 'That looks pretty awesome.'

We could only agree. In front of us were the quietly flowing waters of the narrow inlet which then spread out into a lake 500 m wide. The lake was lined with a mixture of native and exotic trees, their reflections giving the small lake a unique charm. I parked the car alongside the end of the inlet, noticing an old station wagon further up the track. As we got out, we saw two guys fishing further up the inlet. We wandered up to them to check if they were happy to share the water.

'Gidday,' said Frank. 'Mind if we get in behind you?'

'Nah, go for it mate,' replied the angler. 'We're just about ready to chuck it in and head home for some breakfast. It's gone a bit quiet and we haven't had a touch for an hour.'

'So you got a couple then?' enquired Frank, putting on his most charming 'I need information' smile.

'Yeah, we got two good fish first thing but they don't seem interested now. You can see the buggers going up but they just aren't taking.'

Just then Robbie called out from further down the inlet, and we went to see what he was on about. Quite clearly silhouetted against the shingle bottom were two large, dark shapes. They seemed to be in spawning mode as they darted around each other, and we could see they had things on their mind other than feeding. Nevertheless, there was a mad dash back to the car and an ensuing scramble to unravel the mess of rods, waders and assorted tackle.

Rory decided to stay near the car and fish the top section of the lake, as it looked like his sort of water. The rest of us spread out along the inlet bank, with Robbie tackling the fish he had spotted. However, despite repeated casting at the two dark shadows, he got no response.

The other two anglers had packed up and gone back to their Te Awa campsite for a late breakfast. This left us the whole of the inlet, which was great except for the distinct lack of cooperation from the fish. You could see them clearly and drift a nymph right past their noses, but there was no response. They weren't spooked by all the attention, they just seemed totally uninterested.

After half an hour, I decided to walk up to the top of the inlet. The water there was much faster, but also very shallow, less than a metre deep. Right at the top was a large, deep pool where water from the pipeline poured into the lake. Graeme had told us that the lake trout ran through the pipeline to spawn in Flaxy Creek. I had a few desultory flicks in the pool but it was hard to get a good drift because of the strong backswirl.

Following the track, I crossed the pipeline and continued down the far side of the inlet. Below where Frank was fishing, I sat down to adjust my rig to better suit the conditions. Off came the indicator, on went a finer tippet, and a small beadhead nymph replaced the double-fly rig. I had read somewhere that spawning fish, although often not feeding, will have a go at a fly that seems to be invading their territory. Rainbows in particular are very aggressive in defence of their little corner of the river, especially when in spawning mode. With new rig duly set up, I advanced towards the bank.

'Hope you've scared them all over my way,' I called to Frank, only a few metres upstream.

'Well, if I have, how will that help you?' he queried, a trace ungenerously I felt. I decided there was a good chance the fish would be avoiding the flailings on the far side so decided to fish close to my bank. There was more cover there, with scrubby trees and toitoi cladding the edge. This, of course, meant every second cast had to be retrieved from plants of varying description, accompanied by unhelpful comments from the far bank about my casting ability, or lack thereof. I persevered manfully, as the cover afforded by the fly-catching vegetation had to have some appeal for the running trout — surely more than the far side could offer, with all the thrashing it was getting.

Finally I managed to overpower the cast the right amount to hook the nymphs to the right, close to the bank. They drifted down only a few centimetres out from the edge. The line seemed to slow just a touch and I raised the rod, more in hope than expectation of a fish. The hope turned to glee as a big rainbow leapt into the air then fell back into the water with a huge splash.

'Gee!' I exclaimed, or words to that effect.

'Good fish, you jammy bugger,' Frank conceded admiringly as he reeled in to free the water for what was likely to be a prolonged fight. Well, he needn't have bothered. Another huge leap saw the rainbow throw the hook. As I was reeling in the loose line, there was a shout from upstream. We looked up to see Robbie fast into a fish in the riffly water nearer the top of the inlet. Pretty soon he was down near us, hanging onto to a seriously bent rod. The fish came out of the water opposite Frank.

'Bloody hell!' he cried. 'That looks about twelve pounds, you jammy bugger.'

No sooner had he spoken than the fish came off. Robbie took it well but we knew he would be hurting, as it would have been his first double-figure fish. He trudged back upstream to try again.

I sorted out my tackle and moved back to the water's edge. Further upstream there was a bit of an indentation where the bank had been cut away. As I parted the foliage there, I saw a movement about a metre out. Peering intently into the sombre water, I saw the shadow of a large trout, feeding actively. It was necessary to retreat downstream to give myself a bit of casting room, and then up went the small beadhead. It dropped in quietly a metre above the lie. As it neared the shadow, I saw the fish move sideways. I tightened. There was that satisfying stop to the upward movement of the rod. Nothing much happened immediately, then the fish slowly started moving downstream.

'Good fish?' enquired Frank, noting the action.

'Could be a double,' I replied confidently.

'Jammy bugger,' said Frank again automatically.

Fish and I settled down to a long, dogged battle, mainly because, as usual, I had left the net in the car and there was nowhere to land my catch. It was twenty minutes later when I had eased the fish 200 m down the lake to a piece of submerged bank where it was possible to bring it ashore. Finally, the fish was flapping on the grass. I estimated the weight at a pound short of the magic 10 — a good fish. Releasing it, I hurried back to my possie, not wanting to miss any action. But too late. Frank was fast into a big fish that was thrashing the water to froth. Eventually he landed a good 3.75 kg rainbow.

That was the signal for some real action. What brought the fish 'on' we will never know, but we managed to hook about ten in the next hour or so — a mixture of rainbows and browns. Most were in excess of 3 kg. Then the action ended, and nothing would induce any more fish to take.

It was about 1.00 pm by now, and this confirmed a commonly held perception that there is often a surge of feeding activity around midday. Some scientists put this down to fish being able to digest food only when their metabolism is at its most active. They believe that during winter the

Fishing the inlet canal.

warmest part of the day may be the only time sufficient metabolic activity is attained. Of course, it may be more a function of subsurface insect activity, with insects moving or hatching only when the sun has warmed the water. Whatever the reason, it always seems to pay to have a fly in the water around midday.

Since that first day at the lake, I have regularly fished the inlet stretch during winter. It fishes best after heavy rainfall, when the colour of the inflowing water is a peaty brown. If you strike it in this condition, you will be assured of some real action and possibly a big fish, but it pays to use a flashier fly than in clearer water. On another June visit, a 5 kg brown fell to one of Joan Ryder's silver-foil Caddis flies. It was such a heavy fish that when it intercepted the nymph, I thought I had struck a snag. I even yanked the rod two or three times to free the fly. Imagine my mortification when the snag started moving. Fortunately, when the inlet water is discoloured, you are able to fish with a heavier breaking strain, and that was my salvation.

The prolonged battle was witnessed by Murray, a local guide, who had a client with him. As the client had not had much luck, Murray was interested to know which fly I was doing so well with. I gave him one of Joan's creations, and he told me later that the novice angler had gone on to catch seven good fish that day, the silver-foil Caddis proving much more effective than a beadhead in the dirty water.

This demonstrated the ease with which spawning fish could be caught when conditions favoured the angler. So next time you hear of heavy rainfall in the Rotorua area, throw the rod in the boot and head for the Flaxy Lakes. If you've never caught a double-figure fish, this might be your best chance.

Silver foil Caddis fly.

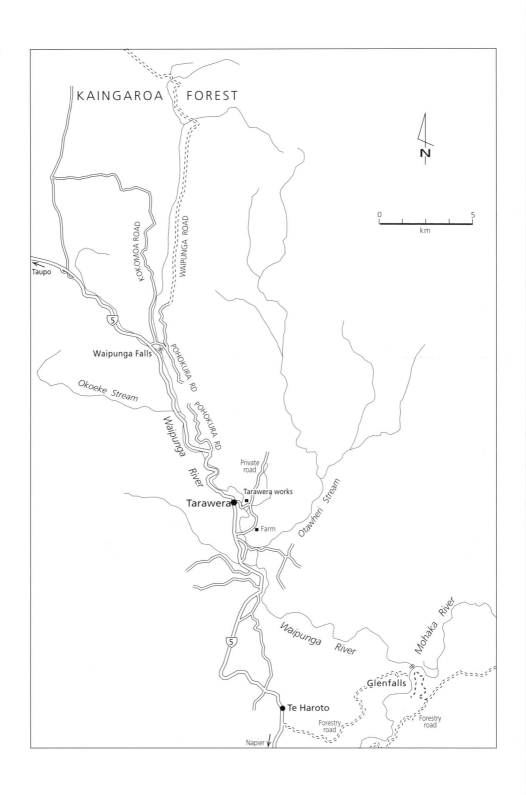

Waipunga River
Matching tactics to the water

DESCRIPTION AND DIRECTIONS

The long journey of this great little river starts high up in the Kaingaroa Forest, the next catchment over from the upper reaches of the Rangitaiki River. The Waipunga, though, flows in the opposite direction; firstly south, until the Waipunga Falls, and then east, until it joins the mighty Mohaka River. It is a river of distinct contrasts. Pine trees envelop the upper reaches, and broom and lupins border the banks. Only brown trout are found in the water above the falls, and they are notoriously difficult to catch. They are worth the trouble, though, as fish of up to 3 kg are to be found.

Access is restricted to two forestry roads on either side of the river, and permission is needed from the Kaingaroa Forest Headquarters. There are several kilometres of fishable water before the river surges over the long drop down the Waipunga Falls. It is here that travellers on the Napier–Taupo road gain their first view of the river, at the popular falls viewing point. Down the hill, the Waipunga is met by the picturesque Okoeke Stream at a car park and picnic spot. For the next 10 km, the main road crosses the river many times. Access is possible at every bridge and at the occasional gap in the bank-side foliage.

In these middle stretches, the river flows through some beautiful native bush with many mature totara towering above their lesser companions. It changes character here, too, as it races down the steep, narrow valley. Gone is the slow, meandering river of the upper reaches: it is now fast and boisterous. Pools are short and sharp, and the best fishing is in the bouldery runs. Progress upstream is confined to wading up the riverbed, as the banks have bush right down to the water's edge. Both rainbow and browns are present, but the former are more prevalent and range from small up to 2 kg. The occasional larger fish is hooked but landing one is a real achievement in this torrent of water.

Further access can be gained from the track behind the Tarawera Tavern (although permission is required), and again from the road on the left just after the old Ministry of Works camp. This road crosses the river and

Waipunga Falls.

continues as a private road to a farm. The water downstream of the bridge yields easier going, but wading the river is possible only if it is low, so access this way can be restricted. Rainbows also tend to be predominant here and range from 0.5 kg to 2.5 kg.

After this access, the river is lost to the road and it is necessary to travel on to the Mohaka. The first road on the left over the river travels several kilometres and catches up with the Mohaka at Glenfalls. Not far past Glenfalls there is a forestry track on the left. A long drive down the hill brings you to a delightful stretch of the big river. Follow the track to its end, and the Waipunga can be seen flowing into the Mohaka at the bottom of a wide, shallow glide. The river can be crossed here in normal flows. Emerging on the south bank of the Waipunga, it is possible to fish for many kilometres upstream. The river here flows through farmland and consists of quite large pools with riffly runs in between. Many hours of productive fishing are possible in these lower reaches, with a mixture of browns and rainbows to be found. The average weight is 1.5 kg, but bigger fish are common, especially during the spawning season.

TALES AND TECHNIQUES

The chuckling waters of the Waipunga River are crossed daily by thousands of vehicles and receive little interest from the majority of passers-by. I was guilty of the same indifference until I persuaded Rory to stop on the way home from a Taupo fishing expedition.

'You've got to be joking!' he exclaimed. 'There's no way you can fish that.'

The subject of his doubt was the torrent below us as we peered over the bridge on the Napier–Taupo road. I had to admit it looked rather daunting. The river was flowing bank to bank, pouring down a narrow valley with no apparent room for an angler to fish the edges. In addition, the banks were thick with blackberry, gorse and other impenetrable foliage.

'Well,' I said, 'I've been reading this book by John Parsons, and he fishes here a lot.'

'What in?' asked Rory. 'A raft?'

Certainly Rory's suggestion made more sense than trying to wade the fierce flow below. I decided I would reread Parsons' book to see if I could get any clues on which section of the river he fished. I had always enjoyed his books, so when I read the Waipunga was his favourite stream, it was a must for me to fish this new water. All we had to do was figure out how to get in it and up it. Further study of Parsons' Waipunga chapters, however, yielded few pointers as to where he went. It was going to be a matter of trial and error, which meant a lot of exploration would be needed.

On my next visit I managed , after a few abortive attempts, to get down into the river at one of the bridges. It was then a matter of slogging my way up the torrent for about six hours to the next bridge. This included grabbing onto toitoi to pull myself up the strong flow, several hairy crossings, some chest-high wades, and negotiating rocks that had the grip of a greased pig. 'Why bother?' I hear you ask. Well, I guess the fact that I hooked fifteen trout of up to 2.75 kg might answer your query. By the time I hauled myself out at the abutments of the next bridge, I was absolutely shattered but could not believe the number of hungry trout that had fastened onto my nymph.

The trout were both brown and rainbow, with rainbow the more abundant. Size ranged from 0.5 kg to 2.75 kg, with an average of around 1.4 kg. Of course, in this river you are lucky to land a third of what you hook. The fighting power of the strong fish in the fast-flowing water is incredible. You have to make an early decision as to whether a fish is worth the effort of dragging it over the slippery boulders maybe 400 m downstream. After a couple of such chases, I learned to yank the fly out of any fish under 1.75 kg, figuring it wasn't worth the slip-sliding charge down the river, trying to hang onto the rod with one hand and the streamside bush with the other. Not to mention the arduous slog back up to where you hooked the fish in the first place. It is necessary to fish with a 3 kg leader, and to bulldoze the smaller ones into the bank before they get out of control, and to keep the pressure on the bigger ones to save you a long walk.

Since those early days, I have fished most of the river from its headwaters in the pine forests right down to the junction with the Mohaka at Glenfalls. These days, I fish the Waipunga with a sense of great familiarity. This comes from knowing the few accesses to the river — where a faint track through the blackberry will not end up in a thicket; where I can scramble up a steep bank to save a long wade up unproductive water; where to drop a fly into the swirling head of a pool to get the most natural drift; where the river can be safely crossed when wading looks impossible; where the always swift current slows just enough to allow a fish to lie; where to cut through the bush to get round a bluff. Such knowledge is the result of many hours spent exploring the river. This has involved trekking up from the mouth a long way through farmland; getting lost in the maze of forest roads while trying to reach a new section of water; risking the wrath of local hunters by using their secret access tracks; and sneaking through the mainly defunct Works camp to get at 'private' waters.

You could never say it was easy fishing. The access is horrific, and unless you are an accomplished bushbasher, some of the stretches are impassable. However, the quality of the fishing makes up for all the pain, and whenever I have had a bad day elsewhere, I know I can always head back to my favourite stretch on the Waipunga and hook enough fish to restore my confidence.

The best stretch I have found is in the middle of the area where the main highway follows the river for several kilometres. Access is gained by picking a way through the blackberry, down a 3 m bank and into the knee-deep water. It is possible to edge along the bank to the bottom of the pool here, but I think it gets a thrashing from the clients of a local guide. For whatever reason, I have never got more than a tiddler out of it. However, the next pool up is a beauty. There is a very deep hole where a large over-hanging willow on the right guards the head. The first lie is two thirds of the way down, where the fish sit in about 1.5 m of water as the main flow loses some of its impetus. All that is required is to chuck a weighted nymph into the centre of the pool and let it drift down, although it usually takes a few casts to get the fly trucking down the centre of the pool where the fish are generally lying.

Typical Waipunga pool.

To get at the deep head of the pool, it is necessary to cross the river, as the willow prevents a cast from the roadside. So long as the river is in normal flow, this crossing is not too bad. I usually wear a pair of stockingfoot 3 mm neoprene waders on the Waipunga. These are waist waders but with a roll-up top that makes them chest high for the occasional deeper crossing. Once across the river, it is an easy right-handed cast straight up the middle of the pool to the rapids at the top. However, if you're left-handed like me, it is a difficult reverse cast. (Why is it that all the best lies are on our wrong casting side? I suspect a conspiracy somewhere.) A heavy sinker nymph is required to get down quickly to the bottom of the pool, and you should be ready for a savage take. The next worry is how to keep a frantic 2 kg rainbow in the pool when it is intent on reaching the safety of the Mohaka River 20 km away.

After that small problem, it is time for the first bushbash of the day. There is a track of sorts that avoids the worst of the blackberry and leads round the big willow to some of the best water on the river. For the next 100 m or so, the stream briefly lets up its headlong charge and the flow is gentler. In the middle of the river is a run 1.5 m deep with many rocks to break the flow — perfect nymphing water. Whenever you see a stretch like this, the expectation level shoots up and the concentration improves. You think, 'Well, if I was a fish, I would think this was a great place to feed.' Usually, two or three trout along there will prove you right.

A worthwhile tactic is to fish the far side of the run for fish lying in the slacker water along the far bank. To do this effectively, it is necessary to lift any loose line out of the water so the leader and indicator drift down at the same speed as the slower current there. Any line left in the faster water will drag the nymph at greater speed, and a wary trout will not look at a nymph travelling faster than the current in which it is lying. The longer your rod, the further you can reach over the faster water to follow the drift of the fly with your arm so you get the maximum drag-free drift. The flash fishing books describe this technique as 'short-lining'. Forget the fancy terms — all you're trying to do is get your fly to come down at the same speed as the water you want to fish.

Having hopefully snared a few trout, it is time to pull your way, toitoi by toitoi, up the side of the stream, bypassing an unproductive stretch of rapids. At the top of the rapids, there is a large boulder with a deep pocket that is worth a cast. One of the biggest fish I have hooked in the Waipunga took hold of my nymph as it swung round the boulder one fine August day. After a few jumps to show me his 4 kg size, he shot into his bolt hole under the boulder and refused to budge. I suppose if you were more patient than I was, you could try to outlast him, but you would have to sit on the rock and commune with nature for a few hours. I'm not convinced the fish would get tired of the wait first.

Once above the rapids, it is time to cross over, as you have reached the 'Neverfail' pool. This is a wide, deep pool reflecting the mature totara that stand guard above. It seems a shame to disturb its perfection, so I sometimes sit down and have lunch at this stage. You can occasionally hear the traffic on the road above, and you wonder how many thousands of people pass by every year ignorant of this little piece of paradise.

'Neverfail' pool.

Piscatorial desires, however, soon overcome aesthetic musings, and it is once more back into the fray. This is an easy pool to fish, and I often reserve it for any visitor who is stupid enough to agree to slog this far up the river with me. The fish are not usually heavier than 1.5 kg, but that is quite enough as they tear off downstream with your unsuspecting guest in hot pursuit yelling for assistance. If you're a harder man than I am, you can leave them to it and probably have an hour or so of uninterrupted fishing. However, as my guests are usually customers this is not a good commercial option, so off I go, net at the ready to shorten the flight downstream of another Waipunga silver bullet.

Having done your good deed, it is time to change to the dry-fly option, as from here up, the Waipunga denizens love a terrestrial floated over their noses. You can either fish the dry on its own or use a combo rig with a dropper nymph trailing a metre below the dry. It is not a good idea to suggest this to a novice fishing companion, however. They will have great difficulty with that split-second decision — whether to count to three if the dry is taken, or to strike immediately if the indicator dry is sunk by a trout taking the nymph below.

I must admit, it took me a few sessions to get my reactions properly programmed into auto-response mode. Yanking the dry out of the trout's mouth with a quick nymphing strike a few times helps drive the lesson home. An added hazard is the willows, which start to overhang the river at this point, and a big Cicada with a weighted nymph trailing behind is not the easiest rig to deliver accurately. This is usually the time I pull out the cheaper bought flies, rather than see my guest lose an hour's worth of personal creations in the willows above.

The last long stretch is the most fun, especially in summer. There are several hundred metres of riffly water, never more than half a metre deep. The best scheme is to wade carefully up the middle of the stream and cast a dry into all the pockets, whether they are along the edges or behind the plentiful rocks. There are many small fish and the occasional 1.5 kg one. They sit in these pockets and just love to wolf down your Grasshopper or Cicada. Just be watchful, though. A few years ago, a large 3.5 kg brown in the very first pocket engulfed my Cicada. It was the largest fish I have landed in the Waipunga and to get it on the dry fly was especially exciting. I know my mates all say I'm a tried and true 'nymphomaniac', but there is nothing more exciting than a big brown erupting from the shallow water to smash your terrestrial. I have had great fun taking visitors with no experience on the dry fly up this stretch. As you quietly plug up

Dry fly pocket water.

the other side of the river, there comes a loud yell from across the way. You turn in time to see a 1.5 kg trout leaping out of the river with a Cicada in its jaw. The sheer joy a first-timer experiences as the trout pounces on their dry fly is a memory you will both treasure for a long time to come.

After a couple of pools at the top of this stretch, you reach the road bridge that marks the end of the day's fishing. If you have made it this far, you will have fished an amazing variety of water, hooked a lot of trout, enjoyed being among mature native bush, and generally marvelled at how such water can be ignored by the hordes on the road above racing through this delightful valley to fish the Taupo rivers.

The Waipunga is a river that demands competence with a range of techniques and a flexibility of approach. If you can adapt to the variety of water encountered, you will catch a lot of fish. But you will be a tired angler as you wade up the last stretch, chucking a big Cicada left and right and reliving the memory of that smashing take by a big brown in the previous riffle.

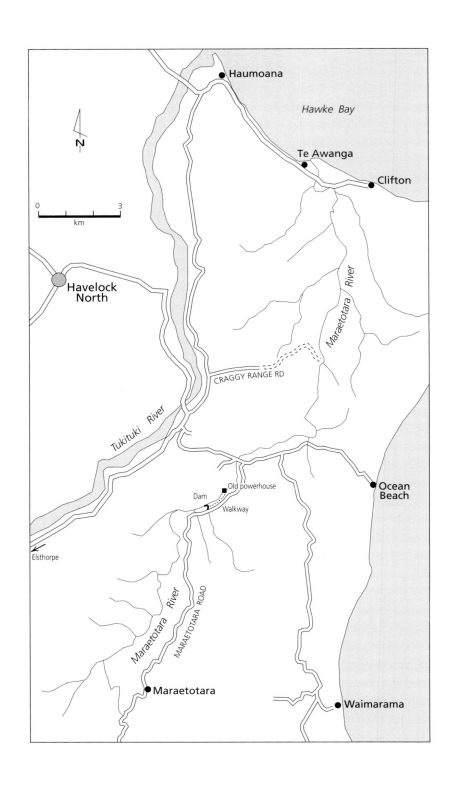

Haumoana

Hawke Bay

Te Awanga

Clifton

Havelock
North

Maraetotara River

CRAGGY RANGE RD

Tukituki River

Old powerhouse

Dam

Walkway

Ocean
Beach

Elsthorpe

Maraetotara River

MARAETOTARA ROAD

Maraetotara

Waimarama

N

0   3
km

Maraetotara River
Techniques for fishing slow water

DESCRIPTION AND DIRECTIONS

This charming, gentle river is a complete contrast to most other Hawke's Bay rivers. Even though it lies just over the hill from the well-known Tukituki River, it is very different in character. This is brown-trout water, making its way quietly between willow-clad banks. For most of its journey it flows through farmland, so access is easy so long as you have permission from the farmer to cross his paddocks.

The Maraetotara River rises on the slopes of Mt Kahuranaki, in the Silver Range, which lies between the Tukituki Valley and the coast at Waimarama. It flows for some 20 km, finally reaching the sea near the township of Te Awanga. Access to the middle and upper reaches is from the Havelock North–Waimarama road. This crosses the river, and just over the bridge, on the right, is Maraetotara Road, which follows the river for several kilometres, although only closely for the first few. There is easy access at the start of the scenic walk 2 km from the turn-off. The walk follows the stream for a few hundred metres up to an old, disused hydro-dam. Below the dam there is a huge pool that often has a good evening rise. Thanks to the dam, the water below here is often fishable when most other Hawke's Bay rivers are in flood.

Above the dam, the Maraetotara is quite small and becomes rather overgrown, but there are significant numbers of fish in the upper reaches for those willing to do some exploring. From Mokopeka Farm on, the road leaves the river and it is necessary to get permission from the local farmers to cross their land. The river is more open along this stretch. As in the lower reaches, the trout are all browns, with an average weight of 1.25 kg.

Below the dam, there is good fishing for several kilometres through the various farms adjoining the river. Access can be gained from Ocean Beach Road for some distance before the river turns left and leaves it. The next access point is at the very end of Craggy Range Road, off Tukituki Road. You will pass a lot of farmlets but keep going until the road runs out. With permission from the farmer at the end, it is possible to go up or down the river for several kilometres in either direction. The river here runs through a deep valley in the middle of farmland. There are clumps of willows but also many stretches with clear banks where stealth is needed to avoid scaring the cruising trout. In some deep pools here, fish up to 4 kg can be seen — especially in the evening. The average weight is a little higher than above the dam — around 1.5 kg.

The only remaining access is at the mouth, at Te Awanga. The road to Clifton crosses the river just after Te Awanga and access is possible through Summerlee and Clifton Stations. However, the lower reaches can get rather shallow, with very few decent pools, and it is necessary to go upstream for some distance to find profitable water. Even so, there often seem to be only small fish this far down. The middle reaches offer better fishing.

The gentle Maraetotara is a pleasant alternative to the bigger, brawling Hawke's Bay rivers, which makes it one not to be missed by visiting anglers.

TALES AND TECHNIQUES

The Maraetotara is a quiet, leisurely stream, and should be approached using tactics to match. I find the more time I spend observing on this river, the more success I have. There is probably a lesson there somewhere.

The first observation came many years ago as I watched an older angler trying to subdue a hard-fighting brown. We were in the middle reaches, not far up from the Waimarama Road, and I had been wandering along the banks trying to spot trout. The wind was howling overhead, and the ruffled surface made spotting hard. I saw the angler ahead and was walking up to him for a yarn when he hooked the fish, but by the time I reached him, it had gone.

'Bad luck,' I consoled.

'More like bad thinking,' he replied. 'I've hooked him before and knew he had that bolt hole under the bank. I just didn't turn him in time.'

'It sounds like you fish here a lot. What are they taking?' I asked.

The old fisherman cocked his head and looked at me for a second or two, seemingly weighing up whether to give away vital information. In the end his ego or generosity got the better of him.

'Willow grub,' he finally said.

'Willow what?' I enquired.

The old fellow sighed and reached down to retrieve his fly. Without comment, he passed a tiny, slim, yellow-bodied nymph to me.

'Never seen one of those before,' I said.

'Well, if you want to fish this river on a windy day, you'd better get some,' he advised. 'They're being blown out of the willows and that's all the trout are interested in. Here, have one,' he offered, taking a nymph from his fly patch.

'Gee, thanks,' I said, as he moved off up the river.

I studied the tiny fly. It was a size 16 by the look of it — admittedly with my very new fly-tier's eye. It seemed to be just ribbed yellow floss with a twist of peacock herl at the top. It didn't look much but I tied it on anyway and moved downstream to a slow patch of water under a mass of overhanging willows. The fly lasted three casts. No, not taken by a huge brown, but securely fastened to a willow branch, 3 m above the pool. The gale had exposed yet another casting deficiency.

Pulling out my fly box, I rummaged through the contents. The only thing that looked remotely yellow was a Greenwell's Glory dry fly. It was about a size 14 so wouldn't be too large, but it wasn't much use with all the wings and hackle. I decided to reduce it to its bare essentials. Stripping off the unwanted adornments, I was left with a greeny-yellow body and a black head. It didn't look very exciting but it would have to do.

Moving up to the head of the pool, where the willows were thinner, I spotted a bulging rise on the far side. A rough sort of roll cast delivered the tatty fly to within a metre of the fish. Another boil came nearby, and I struck. A strong 2 kg Maraetotara brown shot up the pool. After a couple of circuits, it pulled off the best escape trick I have seen in many years of fishing since. Racing up the far side of the pool alongside the bank, it went under a half-submerged branch before leaping a metre straight up in the air. The flimsy leader snapped immediately. I felt like giving the performance a standing ovation. I'm not sure whether the trout had used that technique before, but it was extremely effective.

Having exhausted my supply of anything resembling a willow grub, that was the last catch of the day. No matter what else I tried, the fish were superselective and didn't want anything else. Naturally, on subsequent summer visits to the river, I have always been sure to take a large supply of the tiny flies.

The willow grubs are taken by the trout just below the surface, so there is no need for any weight on the fly. It can be fished as a dry fly, but a better method is the one made famous by G.M. Skues and detailed in his

Willow Grub

Hook: size 14–18, short shank
Tail: none
Body: yellow floss, starting halfway round the bend of the hook
Ribbing: black thread
Head: one herl of peacock

book *Nymph Fishing for Chalk Stream Trout*. Skues is recognised as the 'father' of nymphing through his use of patterns that imitated sub-surface insects. The success of this highly productive fishing method led to many heated debates between the new 'nymphers' and the traditional 'dry-fly only' fishers, led by F.M. Halford. Some of the more famous English trout streams even went so far as banning nymphing, as the method was regarded as morally inferior to dry-fly fishing. After a few years, however, everyone accepted that, as nymphing was based on the exact matching of natural subsurface insects, it required even more skill than dry-fly fishing. Still, Halford went to his grave insisting that nymphing was cheating and against all the principles of honest fly-fishing. Perhaps he would have been more reasonable had he read the words of Roderick Haig-Brown, who wrote: 'All methods of flyfishing are good; each is superior in its own place and time, under its own ideal conditions, to the others; not only superior in effectiveness, but in the pleasure and satisfaction that one derives from fishing it. None is invariably more difficult, more subtle, more artistic or more worthwhile than the others.'

The Skues method involves greasing the leader up to 30 cm or so from the nymph and casting above a 'bulging' trout, i.e. one rising to the fly without breaking the surface during the take. The fish is always sighted, and the angler casts sufficiently above the trout to allow the nymph to sink to the depth of the fish. The take is detected by the movement of the greased part of the leader. This 'greased-cast' method is ideally suited to the Willow Grub. Whenever you are on a willow-lined river on a windy day in summer, this fly should be your first choice. If the trout are feeding on it, they tend to ignore everything else on offer, which can be frustrating if you are not in the know. It is similar to those times in November/ December when the trout take only green beetles and ignore anything that doesn't have a green back.

I remember receiving a hard lesson on this aspect of trout fussiness on the upper reaches of the Ripia River. I had treated my Swiss mate Walter to a weekend's fishing, as I thought it was time he progressed from the easier trout in the nearby Waipunga River. We were fishing on the private waters belonging to a hunting/fishing lodge run by a local Maori trust. Some rather vague instructions from our young host saw us bushbashing for an hour and a half through serious manuka scrub before we reached the stream. It was delightful water that immediately looked 'fishy', and so it proved. There was at least one reasonably sized brown trout in every pool, but catching them was a different story. They were actively feeding — we could see them moving constantly to intercept something subsurface — but we just couldn't figure out what they were taking.

After twenty pools and twenty rejections, I finally fluked a good fish on a 'flashback' Hare'n'Copper. It had been a few years since I had kept a fish, but I decided this one could grace the dinner table in the interests of piscatorial research. I sliced open the belly and out spewed hundreds of

A slow pool on the middle Maraetotara.

green beetles. This was quite a surprise, as it was only October and usually the greens didn't appear until November or December. The fish had been lying in a riffle and had not had time to inspect the fly as closely as his downstream mates. The greeny tinge of the pearl Flashabou had been enough to fool him into thinking it was a green beetle. A quick rummage through the fly box produced a few Green Beetle nymphs tucked away since the previous December, and on they went. Results were immediately forthcoming. Now every pool saw a quick and positive response to the drift-through of the green beetle fly. We caught several sizeable fish but unfortunately, all too soon, we ran out of pools as we reached the point where we had to take the track back to the lodge.

It always pays to have a variety of these 'seasonable' aquatic insects on hand just in case the season arrives unexpectedly. You may read that it is 'green beetle time', but if the beetle has not yet arrived on the river, you will need to try something else fairly quickly. It could be that the brown beetles are hanging around longer than expected and the greens are slower to hatch that year. 'Specific-season' flies of this kind include Brown Beetle, Green Beetle, Willow Grub and Cicada. It is noticeable that the slower the water, the more selective trout can be; in which case it is even more critical to have the right fly. Once you have figured that out, it is a matter of deciding how to fish slow water.

In the middle reaches of the Maraetotara, there are several slow pools. They can be frustrating to fish if you are like me and always thinking about what's around the next corner. When you come across a long, slow pool on this river, it pays to throttle back and take your time. The best approach is to find a good vantage point with some suitable cover from which you can inspect the water. Unless there is a hatch going on, there is unlikely to be much surface activity. If you wait long enough, you will probably see a trout cruising along the bank or in among the weeds. The problem you have to overcome is that of the slow water giving the trout time to have a good long look at your fly. If it is not similar to the naturals drifting past, you are unlikely to get any response. In addition to the 'seasonable' flies, it pays to have a variety of 'slow-water' flies to experiment with, such as Pheasant Tail nymphs and several Caddis imitations. Generally, the slower the water, the more exact your imitation needs to be. As the Maraetotara flows mainly through farmlands, much of it is slow.

Farms can produce another problem, as Rory once found out. He was fishing the good stretch of water through the farm at the end of Craggy Range Road. Hiding behind a large willow, he was concentrating on spotting fish when he noticed a movement from the corner of his eye. He turned to find a large bull steadily moving towards him down the farm track. He watched the bull advancing, and when it started snorting, figured it was time to move. In front of him was a large pool, with the river too deep to cross. The only salvation was the willow tree above. Clutching his rod in one hand, he clambered up — and none too soon, as the red-eyed bull arrived only a moment later and started butting the tree, still snorting away. Rory moved out onto a slender limb, which bent alarmingly but was at least well out of reach of the bull. This impasse was to continue for an hour and a half — Rory on branch and bull at foot of tree.

While Rory was up there, motionless for fear of breaking the branch, several trout swam by. Unfortunately the foliage was too thick and his perch too precarious for Rory to get a fly down to the water. Even if he had managed this, I am not sure how he would have landed a fish. It would have rated as one of the most meritorious catches of all time. He would probably have had to use the technique of 'dapping'. Originating in England, and used there with a dry fly, this is very useful when there is little casting room, as is often the case on willow-infested rivers like the Maraetotara.

The idea is to study the trout's movements for some time. If it is on a cruising beat, you need to position yourself halfway along and, most importantly, find some cover. This may be behind a bush, up a tree or even lying down on the bank where it overhangs the pool. It is necessary to remove any indicator and wind the fly up to near the top ring of the rod. After the fish swims by, gingerly manoeuvre the rod through the dense foliage. Once it is out over the water, you can carefully lower the nymph with a gentle shake of the rod, then allow it to sink to the depth at which the trout is cruising.

In a gentle current, it is possible to follow the nymph's slow drift down the stream with the rod tip. Be ready for the return trip, as the fish is quite likely to investigate your offering on the way back. If it ignores the fly on the way downstream, lift out the nymph and swing the rod back upstream as far as you can. Lower the fly in again and wait for the fish to return. If it looks like passing by a second time, give the fly some motion by lifting it a little or twitching it. This may be enough to attract the trout's interest. Of course, your chances of landing the fish, enshrouded as you are in tree or bush, may not be great, but at least you will have had some excitement.

Fishing the Maraetotara River may require developing some new techniques (apart from dodging bulls) to catch the selective trout you will find

Dapping.

in its gentle waters. However, the experience will prove invaluable when you come to test your skills on such famous rivers as the Motueka or the Mataura. Then all the time spent developing your slow-water techniques should pay off big time.

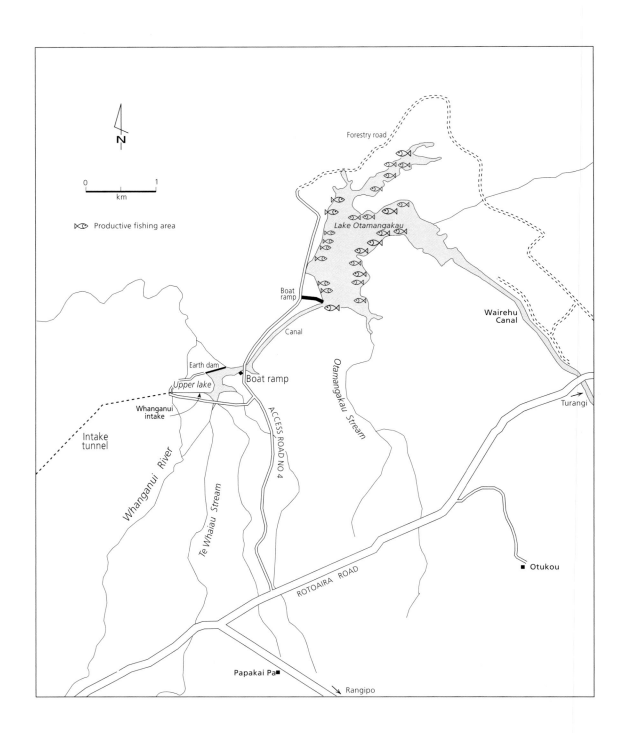

Lake Otamangakau
Lake-fishing techniques

DESCRIPTION AND DIRECTIONS

Lake Otamangakau is a typical example of a 'drowned' hydro-lake, i.e. a lake formed as part of a major hydroelectricity scheme. In that sense it is similar to Lake Aniwhenua and the more recently created Lake Dunstan. It lies on the central plateau between Turangi and Mt Ruapehu, and is reached from SH 47. There is an access road off the road to Turangi, not far from the SH 47 junction at Papakai.

Otamangakau was formed in 1971 by diverting the waters of the upper Whanganui and Whakapapa rivers through a pipeline that feeds into a small upper lake, retained by an earth dam. Not far down from the end of the pipeline, Te Whaiau Stream enters the top lake. This is the major spawning stream for all of Lake Otamangakau. There is a gravel road that crosses the stream and continues over the end of the incoming pipeline. Access can be gained from here to the other side of the top lake, and there is a good hole at the end of the point. The other recommended area is a very productive deep riffle just below where the stream meets the inlet waters.

The best fishing in the upper lake is after heavy rainfall in the Whanganui catchment any time in autumn or early winter, up to the season's close on 30 June. Any increase in volume or discolouration of the incoming water triggers the spawning urge, and the Otamangakau fish head up the inlet canal. Both rainbows and browns are caught here, with an average weight close to 2 kg.

Back on the road to the main lake, there is a bridge over the inlet canal that flows from the upper to the main lake. Just before the bridge, a road to the left leads to a boat ramp. There is good fishing right off the boat ramp itself. After the bridge, the main road continues to the earth dam. On the right before the dam is the main boat ramp. From here, it is possible to walk round to the point where the inlet canal flows into the river — a good night-fishing spot.

The access road continues round the lake with pine forest on the left and mainly unattractive, scrubby growth near the water. It is more the lake's isolation and a mountain surround that give it appeal. A sharp eye is needed to spot the tracks heading off from the road down to the lake edge. Some of these need a 4WD, especially in wet conditions. The road then veers away from the river heading to the north of the lake. Another access road goes off to the right and eventually follows the exit canal taking the water to Lake Rotaira and through the hill to the Tokaanu Power Station.

Mouth of Te Whaiau Stream.

Lake Otamangakau covers about 2 sq km but has an average depth of only 2.5 m. There is a deeper channel in the middle of the lake but the maximum depth is around only 10 m. This makes for pleasant fishing from a boat, as heavy gear is not required, although strong leaders are needed as trout up to 9 kg have been caught. The average is just under 2 kg, and both browns and rainbows are present. Rainbows are caught more frequently, but that may simply reflect the difficulty of catching the more wary browns. The lake is notorious for being difficult, and blank days are common. However, the size and quality of the elusive Otamangakau trout make the effort worthwhile — a double-figure fish is always a possibility.

TALES AND TECHNIQUES

The Big O — as Lake Otamangakau is frequently called — holds a special memory for me, as it was the place where I caught my first legal trout. I was introduced to the lake by an old cricket mate Austin Harris. He was a trout-fishing fanatic and had chucked in life in the big smoke to settle in Turangi. He was well known around the fishing town for the things he got up to in the pursuit of the really big one.

Austin's most famous trick was to park by the road bridge over the Tokaanu outlet canal, then proceed to undress down to his boxers. Anyone looking on could be excused for thinking he was doing a 'Reggie Perrin' and was about to end it all. But instead, he would enter the water holding his clothes and rod over his head and dog-paddle 150 m to the middle pier of the bridge. The current is not fierce, but it was still a pretty good effort to get there using only one arm. He would then climb onto the base of the pier, dress and begin fishing for the huge trout that fed on the chopped-up food coming down from the powerhouse turbines. Of course, he landed only those fish that chose to cooperate, as his options for following the fish down the canal were rather limited. Still, Austin always ended up with a trout or two, as well as a story about the huge one he had not been able to convince to come back upcurrent.

These forays went well for some time, until Austin was persuaded by a nephew to take him to a 'real good possie'. Having checked the sixteen-year-old could swim, Austin took him to Tokaanu, and the pair of intrepid anglers launched themselves into the cold waters of the canal. It wasn't long before Austin realised his nephew's estimation of his swimming abilities had been somewhat overrated. Austin was forced to cast his rod and clothes aside to rescue the struggling youth and drag him to the shore. Needless to say, future expeditions never included company again.

As he was always chasing big trout, Austin was a regular visitor to the Big O. Mostly he preferred to fish the moving water of the inlet canal rather than the still waters of the lake itself. He showed me how to start fishing from the boat ramp on the upper lake and work round up to the head of the intake. I distinctly remember one wintry day in May when the usual Otamangakau wind was howling into our faces as we stood together, casting off the boat ramp.

I had recently acquired a graphite rod, still something of a newfangled invention at the time. Despite the benefits of modern technology, I was struggling to get out more than 10 m of line. This was due probably as much to a lack of expertise as to the strong wind. Meanwhile, Austin was wielding his trusty old Fenwick fibreglass rod with a skill that comes naturally to only a few. He would make a leisurely back cast, commune with nature for a while as the line unfurled, then effortlessly punch the slow-action rod into the gale. Out would stream about 25 m of line, seemingly unaffected by the wind. I always reckoned he had time to smoke a cigarette while he waited for his back cast to straighten.

Austin had taken me up the inlet canal on that first visit, and I had watched as he hooked several trout up to 3.5 kg on the nymph. My efforts had gone unrewarded on that occasion, but I was determined to return, as it had seemed an appropriate spot for a novice. I managed to convince my family that Tokaanu would be a great place for a holiday, and Easter Saturday saw me back on the launching ramp. For once the dreaded Otamangakau wind was absent, and I was able to cast a reasonable distance away from the shore. It was not too long before Austin's tuition paid off and a well-conditioned 3 kg rainbow came to the net.

One thing you always notice about Otamangakau trout is their fighting spirit. One of the guys from Tisdalls who was brought up in the area always insisted a strain of steelhead had been released into the Whanganui River years before. He maintained these trout were easily differentiated from rainbows by their dark-green backs and the fight they put up. His theory was that the steelhead had reached the lake through the pipeline that diverts the headwater flow of the Whanganui River into Lake Otamangakau via the inlet canal.

Up until twenty years ago, most experts believed New Zealand rainbow trout had their origins in the Russian River in California. As that was once a famous steelhead river, it seemed the theory could have some factual basis. It has since been proven, however, that the original 1883 shipment in fact came from a hatchery on the Sonoma Creek in the Napa area, now famous for its wines. Nevertheless, there is now considerable debate as to whether there was just a single shipment in 1883, as some evidence points to later shipments from the McCloud and Shasta rivers in California — both steelhead rivers. It has not been established just what those shipments might have consisted of, or where the resulting fry were released. Jack McKenzie, of Rangitikei River fame, is convinced the Rangitikei rainbows are a steelhead strain from the McCloud River. If a shipment reached the Rangitikei, who can say for sure that a shipment of steelhead did not get through to the Whanganui River?

There are also many anglers who believe the rainbows of the Ruakituri are also a steelhead strain, and anyone who has fastened onto one of those 'bulldozers' would agree they are something special. That particular strain of trout is now being released in other waters around New Zealand, so we can expect to encounter more of these hard-fighting fish as they take hold in areas outside the Urewera. Recent evidence indicates New Zealand also received a strain of trout from Kootenay Lake in British Columbia — the Gerard strain — known for its large size and rapid growth, just like Otamangakau trout.

It is a fact that Otamangakau trout grow very big, very quickly, but whether this is a matter of feed or origin is open to debate. Originally it was believed 'drowned' lakes such as Otamangakau and Aniwhenua produced big trout for a few years while the subsurface insect life was abundant. The phenomenal growth rates then tapered off as the food source declined. Now that both lakes are well past this stage and still producing trophy trout, it makes one wonder just what accounts for the high growth rates. We can safely leave this to the scientists to ponder while we enjoy the end result.

There are many ways of fishing the Big O apart from blind-nymphing the inlet canal. One of the most common is to use a boat to get out from the shore and cast back to the weed beds. A slow-sinking or tip-sinking line is most effective, and the damselfly- or dragonfly-nymph imitations are usually productive (if the fish are biting). There is a deeper channel that meanders along the lakebed to the outlet, and fishing along the edges of this can be quite rewarding, especially in the heat of summer.

The lake can be fished from the bank, from where large browns may be sighted cruising the patches between the weeds. They sometimes cruise so shallowly that their fins are out of the water. If the lake is not too high, you can wade out to fish the deeper water beyond the weed beds, where the rainbows are more prevalent. Fish scientists believe the more aggressive browns tend to scare the rainbows away from the food-rich shallower areas. It therefore pays to make sure you have fished the weed beds first or you may miss out on that big cruising brown. Float-tubing is a productive way of fishing this deeper water without scaring the trout, and a lot of shoreline can be covered in a day. Lately the one-man rubber duckies have become popular and are a lot cheaper than a sophisticated float tube — and you don't need to buy a wet suit.

Fish can be caught anywhere around the shore, and the most successful areas are shown on the sketch map. But, bear in mind, Otamangakau trout are hard to catch. The average success rate is around one fish per day for the visiting angler, although some of the locals do a lot better. In fact one was reported to have caught as many as 331 trout in two months in 1997. This was probably over summer, when the Big O becomes a mecca for dry-fly and big-fish aficionados.

Summer is the time for the Cicada. This favourite trout morsel usually emerges from its larval form in the swampy land surrounding the lake in

January or February. It is always hard to know just when cicadas will hatch, as it depends greatly on the weather. It pays to check with local tackle shops if the hatch is 'on' or not. If you manage to strike it lucky, the fishing can be really hot, compared with the usual miserly Otamangakau success rate. Any type of Cicada pattern will do, but it helps to have a few different body colours available in case you get refusals with one particular colour. I find Norman Marsh's Cicada pattern (as described in *Trout Stream Insects of New Zealand*) is usually effective, but any of the commercial patterns will do just as well. Although the natural insect has a greeny-black body, the neutral colour of the deer-hair Cicada pattern still seems to work. If you are concerned about body colour, you can always adopt the approach of many American fly-fishers and take along a selection of felt-tipped markers to colour your fly as appropriate on the day.

You might find the fish concentrate more on the silhouette of the fly sitting on the water than details such as colour. Several angling writers have noted that in still-water fishing it is more important that the silhouette is close to the natural than that the fly be a perfect all-round representation. This is proven by the success of the Cicada patterns that do not have wings, which seem to work as well as the winged versions. I admit I like the look of the winged Cicadas, probably because I admire the skill of the fly-tier in producing such a complicated fly.

If the hatch is on, the fishing is relatively easy so long as you keep a low profile as you stalk the weed beds. When you spot a rising trout, just chuck the Cicada near it. A slightly splashy presentation will tend to draw the trout's attention rather than scare it off, so you don't need to be a perfect caster. All terrestrial flies should hit the water with a bit of a splash so the trout notices the tasty new morsel. If the initial impact fails to attract the fish, an occasional twitch may do the trick. It is essential to give your Cicada some action, as trout prefer their food live.

A splashy presentation can also work subsurface. Toss a beadhead nymph a few metres out and the plop will similarly alert the trout that a tasty treat is on the way down. Allow the nymph to sink, then retrieve it with a slow, jerky action, varying the speed. The take will probably come at the edge of the weed beds. A longer rod will enable you to lift the fly clear without getting entangled in the weed. A rod length of around 3 m will give you an advantage.

Any of the usual beadhead patterns will work, although the slimmer ones, such as the CDC versions, seem to do better than the fast-water varieties like a Hare'n'Copper. However, the most consistent producer is a beadhead Damselfly, as damselflies form a major part of the Big O trout diet. Damselfly nymph patterns vary considerably, but the one described has worked well at Otamangakau.

This fly should be retrieved with a more random jerky movement as damselfly nymphs swim with a distinctive wiggle. If your fly-tying is up to making a 'wiggle' nymph, you will get a better imitation of the natural insect's movement.

Another very successful Otamangakau fly is the Olive Nymph, a general imitation of snails and also damselflies. Snails are an important part of the diet of an Otamangakau fish. However, there are few patterns that duplicate the shape of a freshwater snail. The Olive Nymph, when fished with a very slow retrieve, is perhaps the best option.

Other flies worth trying include the more typical lake-fishing ones, such as unweighted traditional 'eyed' Damselflies or Red Midge Pupas on a slow-sinking line. If these don't

Beadhead Damselfly

Hook: size 8–12, long shank
Tail: three olive-green hackle tips tied so they lie flat on the water
Abdomen: olive-green seal's fur or substitute
Ribbing: fine gold wire
Thorax: as for abdomen but tied bulkier
Wing-case: olive goose or similar
Hackle: olive-dyed partridge
Head: gold bead

work, put on a beadhead version of the same pattern, as this will often bring a change of luck. Weighted versions, like the beadheads, work best with a lift-and-draw technique. Allow the nymph to sink, then slowly raise the rod tip from horizontal to vertical before lowering the tip while retrieving the loose line. This imitates the languid rise to the surface of an emerging nymph, and the take usually comes as the nymph sinks back, so you need to be in contact with the fly at all times. Be extra vigilant as the fly sinks down from your cast, as there will often be a gentle take on the way down. This is hard to detect, and you need to be very watchful or you will miss the slight pause in the sinking rate. This is where the expert lake fisherman has the advantage over someone more used to moving-water takes.

If you are more of a river fisherman, you might find the easiest time to catch an Otamangakau trout is during one of the cicada hatches. If the prospect of a one-handed dog-paddle across the Tokaanu Canal does not appeal, Cicada time on the Big O might well be the way to go.

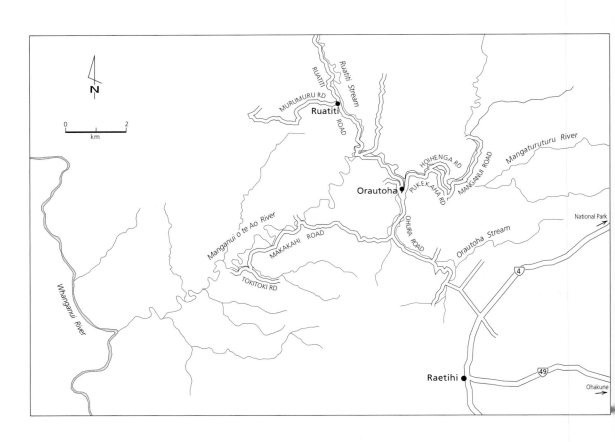

Manganui o te Ao River
Fishing swirling pools

DESCRIPTION AND DIRECTIONS

The Manganui o te Ao is a superb back-country river, and rightly protected by a National Water conservation order. The only problem is getting to it. Perhaps as little as 10 per cent of the river can be reached on foot. There is only one access road, Ohura Road, which crosses the river at Ruatiti. Apart from a couple of side-roads off this, the river can be fished only from raft or canoe as it flows between high cliffs on its way to join the Whanganui north of Pipiriki. The side-roads provide access to two sections: Manganui Valley Road gets you to the water upstream of Ruatiti, Makakahi Road to water further down.

The upper section can be reached by crossing farm paddocks when you have gained permission from the usually friendly farmers. There is a notice-board at the Ruatiti Domain that gives details of the farm boundaries and the contacts for each farm. But even from these few access points, getting down to the river is the problem. The road runs along the ridge above and only rarely drops down to anywhere near the water. In most places the road and farmland are high up, with a sheer drop down perpendicular papa cliffs to the river. Be careful bushbashing as you may find the next step takes you 50 m further down.

Where the river can be reached, it is possible to forge up the gorges only in midsummer. Even then the crossings are waist deep — not dangerous, as the water at the tail of the pools is slow, but rather cool work, even in summer. During the rest of the year, you may be able to make your way up only a couple of pools or so before it becomes too deep to cross.

There is better access on the far (north) side of the river. Here the farmland regularly dips down to the water's edge, and it is possible to hop from pool to pool via the paddocks. There are bridges across the river on Pukekaha Road and again further down on Hoihenga Road. In this area, a drift/dive count has found around twenty medium-to-large trout per kilometre, mainly rainbows. Rainbows range in weight from around 0.5 kg to about 3 kg, with an average of around 1.5 kg. Browns start at around 1 kg and also go up to 3 kg, with a similar average. There is the occasional bigger fish, most likely to be encountered in the evening.

In the Ruatiti area, the Manganui o te Ao is a big river with wide rapids and forbiddingly deep pools. Drift/dive surveys have revealed a substantial population of around 40 medium-to-large trout per kilometre. Brown trout tend to predominate from Ruatiti down. To fish below Ruatiti, turn off Ohura Road at Makakahi Road. A few kilometres down here, a farm bridge crosses the river. It is possible to fish a kilometre or so upstream, depending on the river level, and, with the farmer's permission, quite a long way downstream. There seems to be more angling pressure in this area, and the trout tend to be smaller than in the upper section, with an average weight of around 1.2 kg. The river is confined by large cliffs and consists of a mixture of big, deep pools and deep, rocky runs. Further down near the end of Makakahi Road, the river can be accessed for the last time before it disappears, heading for its junction with the Whanganui River 10 km away.

TALES AND TECHNIQUES

If you are tramping or skiing on the western slopes of Mt Ruapehu, pause for a moment and look out west. On a clear day, you will be able to see Mt Taranaki and, starting at the Ruapehu foothills, a deep chasm that seems to lead towards the west coast. Maori legend tells how Taranaki used to stand with the other central North Island mountains — Tongariro, Ruapehu and Ngauruhoe. All was fine between them until Tongariro caught Taranaki with his wife, Pihanga, and forced Taranaki to flee to the west. The deep furrow left by his passing is the valley through which the beautiful Manganui o te Ao River now flows.

The river has its origins high on the slopes of Mt Ruapehu, and the cool water provided by the melting snow provides ideal trout habitat further downstream. Unfortunately the recent volcanic activity of Ruapehu has deposited ash in the rivers draining the mountain, and this has resulted in increased mineralisation, which is not good for trout. Most of the worst-affected water comes from the Mangaturuturu River, causing a lot of sedimentation immediately downstream of the confluence, which has resulted in a loss of nymph life, so it is best to fish well down from here. In the middle reaches rainbows tend to lie in the faster water and browns in the pools, as you would expect. However, the browns do not lie in the heart of the pools, even if the current is slow. Their favourite trick is to lie in the backswirl. Here they can sit in comparative comfort, with the main flow coursing past while the gentle backflow brings them plenty of food without their having to expend much energy. Trout are energy-conscious, and this backswirl lie is a typical example of how they seek out the most efficient position to balance food source and energy use.

I have encountered similar positioning by browns on the Mohaka River. On one early Mohaka excursion, I remember working my way up from the Waipunga confluence and reaching the cliffs at the head of the valley. Where the full force of the river met the base of the cliffs, the river cannoned off and charged down the centre of the valley. At the edge of this flow was a swirl of water making its way back upstream to the head of the pool. I tried to fish the seam where the fast water met the slow, but the nymph was either swept down the river or went nowhere in the backswirl. Frustrated that I could not get the drift I wanted, I pulled the line out of the fast water and let it dangle in the slow. The fly line started to come upstream towards me, carried by the backswirling flow towards the top of the pool.

A serene pool on the Manganui o te Ao.

As the fly came near, I lifted the rod to recast. It got about halfway, then stopped. I was into a fish — but only briefly. The unexpected take had caught me by surprise, and the fish was not well hooked. The fly came back to me fishless, but I had stumbled on a new technique.

I moved up to the next pool, which was similar to the one I had just fished, and cast downriver into the backswirl heading towards me. Good theory, but nothing happened. Then, on the second attempt, the indicator seemed to hesitate just as it reached the head of the pool. I wasn't sure what was happening but I lifted the rod, more in hope than in expectation, to find myself fast into another brown, and before long I had landed a 2.5 kg fish. I quickly figured out the fish were facing downstream and so needed a different approach to the standard upstream nymphing method.

The main problem with this technique is the take tends to come at the top of the backswirl. If the fish takes partway up, it is just like a normal drift and you strike at the stopping of the indicator. But if nothing happens before the fly reaches the point where the current starts to head downstream again, you're in trouble. The fly line tends to swim around at the top of the backswirl, going nowhere in particular, and it is virtually impossible to detect a take. You may fluke a few, but they will usually be poorly hooked and a lost fish is likely. In addition, you tend to look a bit silly to a fellow nympher observing from the far bank, as you are facing down the river instead of up. However, when you lift the rod on a big brown, you can flash them a knowing look.

On the Waitahanui River in Taupo, I often used to notice the odd angler facing the 'wrong' way while nymphing. It wasn't until I fished the river with my mate Frank that I found out what they were doing. Frank took me to a pool he had nicknamed the 'Broken Jaw Pool'. The name came from an encounter with a trout with a malformed jaw. It was a wide pool, with a shingle ledge up the middle at about knee depth. Frank waded out purposefully through the strong current to the ledge. He cast to the side of the pool, where there seemed to be a confused current. After a couple of attempts, he got the nymph in the right place and it moved steadily upstream, along the edge of the overgrown bank. When the fly reached the top of the pool, it started moving back down again with the force of the main current. With one cast, Frank had fished both up and down the pool. A couple of circuits later, a 2 kg rainbow took the nymph as it was drifting along under the bank and tore off downstream.

Hooking a fish in the Waitahanui is always the least of your problems. Frank beckoned me to take over his possie while he did battle with the fish further downstream. It took me quite a while to get just the right cast to place the fly in the backflowing current. It was then necessary to mend line upstream ahead of the indicator, contrary to the usual procedure. This way, the fly line could be guided along the bank so as not to hold back the fly and give an unnatural drift.

On the Manganui o te Ao, you have to do something similar if you want to fish up the backswirl and back down again. As the fly swings round and starts the return journey, it is necessary to get the line out of the water flowing in the opposite direction. You then need to roll-cast a metre of line ahead of the indicator to get the nymph moving back down, otherwise it will just sit motionless in the middle of the backswirl.

Once the fly starts trucking down the edge of the main current, it is a matter of keeping the belly of the fly line away from the water flowing in the opposite direction. If the seam water is less than 3–4 m away, you can do this by just lifting your rod and all the line off the water. This leaves only the 50 cm 'bow' of your line near the indicator on the water. You should then follow the movement of the indicator with your rod. When the rod has reached its full arm's-length reach, feed some more line through the rings to get another metre or two of dead drift. In a backswirling pool, the line will start coming back upstream towards you and you can retrieve line as you would with a normal drift. It all sounds complicated, but once you master the downstream mend, you can fish a pool both up and down with one cast — and a few mends.

During the heat of the day on the Manganui o te Ao, this is often the only method that works. If you fish the pools conventionally, by casting into the eye of the pool and drifting the nymph through, you are likely to pick up only small rainbows. The fish don't seem to lie where you would expect them. Whether they are particularly lazy, I don't know, but in the backswirl of the pool is where they prefer to lie. I never did very well on this river until I discovered this quirk of trout behaviour. I used to pick up the odd fish, mainly from pocket water, but rarely from the pools. Since I started concentrating on fishing the backswirls, I have usually managed four or five fish in a day.

Only once have I done much better than that. It was on an expedition to the river in midsummer. Driving along Pukekaha Road, I noticed a new slip had spewed clay across the road. It had since been cleared and the debris bulldozed over the bank and down into the paddocks. The clay spoil had helpfully covered up the blackberry and other undergrowth that would otherwise have been impenetrable. By scrambling down the slip, I

Main current →

Fast →

Fly →

← Slow

Downstream mending.

got to a section of river I had not fished before.

The first three pools each yielded a fish from their backswirl — two browns and a rainbow, all around 1.5 kg. It was a good start, considering I had reached the river only around 11.00 a.m. on a stinking hot, breathless February day. Further up, after a rather wet crossing, I came to a stunning pool all of 200 m long. It was the only deep rocky run I had ever found on the river. The bottom was 1–2 m deep and strewn with stones, rocks and the odd big boulder. The current was slowish and there was no backswirl to worry about, as the river flowed unusually straight for the whole length of the pool. I could, for a change, spot my quarry and cast to the trout. Fish of two and three kilos were actively feeding despite the heat of the day. I spotted six and hooked four of them, and another two took in the head of the rapids at the top.

Days such as this are rare on the Manganui o te Ao, and it was enjoyable to get back to normal 'sighted-fish' angling. The killer fly of the day was a size 14 beadhead Pheasant Tail. On bright days, I like to use the original Sawyer tie, in which the thorax consists solely of wound copper wire. This gives a nice bright flash as the sunlight catches the copper and seems to get the fish out of their midday stupor.

This is a pattern that will work anywhere you turn over a rock and find small brown mayfly nymphs clinging to the undersurface. These nymphs are found throughout the country, so there should be some Pheasant Tail nymphs in every New Zealand fly box.

Halfway up the long run, my concentration was broken by the antics of a Blue Duck as it tried to scramble up the papa rock on the far bank. I wasn't sure if it was trying to reach its nest or divert my attention from its nearby ducklings. Wings flapping, feet scrabbling, it struggled for a footing on the bare rock face, but kept falling just short of the scrubby ledge above and sliding on its tummy back down into the water. Finally, it made a supreme effort and gained the safety of the ledge and disappeared into the undergrowth — so its nest must have been there, I decided. The blue mountain duck is a regular sight on the Manganui o te Ao, as the species is protected. They are now present in good numbers, and their strange cry can be heard on any stretch of the river.

On that magic day, I sat on a boulder eating a late lunch, listening to the birds and watching the crystal-clear water flowing down the bush-lined run. There are few rivers in New Zealand that can match the beauty of the Manganui o te Ao as it flows quietly through the sombre native bush. With only the cry of the blue duck to disturb the solitude, it was easy to ignore the fish for a while and simply absorb the beauty around me. Sometimes we are so busy fishing we forget why we are drawn to such places. To be on rivers like this is the reason we fish, and we should treasure each moment there. The fish are just a bonus!

Sawyer Pheasant Tail

Tail: few whisks of cock pheasant tail
Body: three or four strands of peacock herl
Ribbing: fine copper wire — can be twisted round the body material if preferred
Thorax: copper wire built up to typical thorax shape
Wing-case/hackle: cock pheasant tail whisks tied in under the copper thorax, then brought forward over the thorax as a wing-case with sufficient length for the ends to form 'legs'
Head: black thread tying off the wing-case and dividing the legs

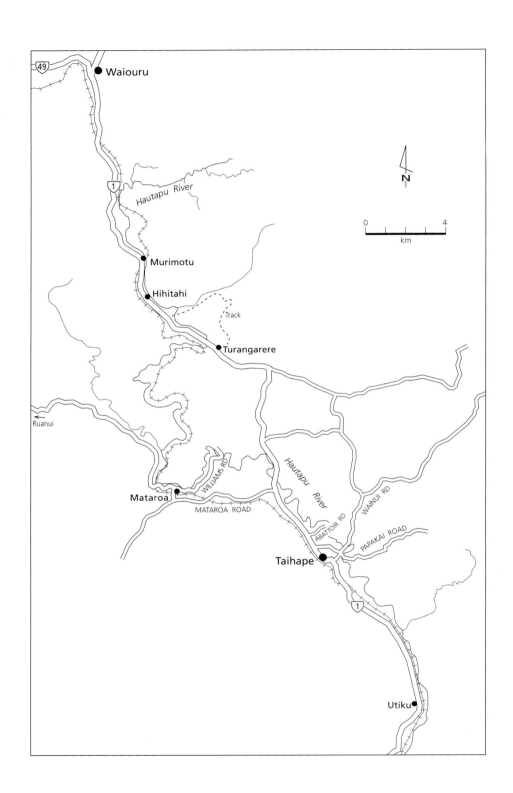

49

Waiouru

1

Hautapu River

Murimotu

Hihitahi

Track

Turangarere

Ruanui

WILLIAMS RD

Mataroa

MATAROA ROAD

Hautapu River

ABATTOIR RD

WAINUI RD

PAPAKAI ROAD

Taihape

1

Utiku

N

0   4
km

Hautapu River
Tactics for cruising browns

DESCRIPTION AND DIRECTIONS

The Hautapu River rises in the hills east of Waiouru. Most of the initial flow comes from the Ngamatea Swamp just south of Waiouru, where the river makes a left-hand turn to flow south through farmland alongside SH1 for two kilometres. The river is quite small at this point, averaging only 2–3 m wide. The bottom is rather silty, especially in the slower pools, but there is the occasional deeper pool giving plenty of cover. A mixture of rapids and slow water makes for a variety of fishing. In summer, the flow decreases and the river gets quite low.

There is easy access to this section from two rest areas beside the road, or any of the various farms through which the river rambles. Leading to the Hihitahi Scenic Reserve there is a designated track that can be used to reach worthwhile water. While the river flows are normal, there are some good fish in this area. They are all brown trout, averaging 1.5 kg but with the odd fish up to 4 kg. However, they are not easy to catch as the exposed nature of the river makes them wary.

The next section starts where the main highway crosses the river for the first time, just south of Hihitahi. Just below the bridge, the river enters a bush-lined gorge. Thanks to the faster water and overhead vegetation, the fishing is a bit easier here, but that also means more angling pressure, which probably accounts for why there are fewer big fish. Outside of sum-mer flows, the gorge can be tough going, as you have to stay in the river most of the way through. The bush is rather dense and the banks very steep, so you need to pick your way along the edge. The best bet is to start at the lower end and climb out at the road bridge. It is then only a 2 km walk back to the car along the busy main road. It takes only half an hour to walk back, but the best part of a fishing day to fish through the gorge. The river here is much the same size as in the upper section, but it flows faster over a rocky bottom and around small boulders — good trout habitat.

After the gorge, the river leaves the main road and flows in a more west-erly direction. You can access this stretch by driving round to Mataroa and turning down Kakariki or Ruanui Road. The lower reaches are heavily willowed and access can be a struggle. There is better water further up under the railway viaduct, where the road veers away from the river, with access through the neighbouring farms. The water here is slower and also silty but with a bouldery bottom that harbours plenty of nymphs. Accordingly, the fish are a reasonable size and in good condition. Several 2–3 kg fish are likely to be sighted during a day's fishing, especially early in the season.

The river rejoins the main road just after the Taihape Golf Club. Downstream the banks are clearer, with only the occasional willow as the river flows through open farmland. This section is not so appealing, as the riverbed is mostly smooth papa rock in which the river has not been able to hollow out any decent holes, so the water is rather shallow and lacks the cover that comes with depth. Access is easily gained down Abattoir Road just before Taihape, and again at Winiata south of Taihape, before the Hautapu joins the Rangitikei near Utiku.

TALES AND TECHNIQUES

The upper Hautapu River.

It probably isn't often that you can say you had to risk your life to go fishing. However, if you want to fish all of the Hautapu River, that is definite-

ly what you have to do. The reason for this is that for part of its course the Hautapu flows through Army land. The Army will, on occasion, allow you to fish their part of the river but insists you sign a waiver. Basically, this says that if you are blown up, it is your fault, not theirs! It would be rather difficult to spot for trout with one eye while watching for incoming Scud missiles with the other. Accordingly, for a review of the fishing in the Army section you will need to find a braver writer than this one.

So far as the rest of the river goes, you'd never say it was the prettiest river you'd ever seen, but it harbours a lot of good-sized brown trout, and that more than compensates for any lack in aesthetics. The top section of the river is best fished early or late in the season. During the low flows of midsummer, the fish tend to drop back to the deeper pools or even down to the Rangitikei River. You will find only the occasional fish during a daytime sortie. They appear to hide during the day and feed only at night, presumably because of the lack of cover. The upper section of the river is a favourite of mine, not just for the quality of the fishing, but because it taught me a crucial fly-fishing lesson.

My worst fault in my early fishing days was that I went about it too fast. For years I had read how important it was to take your time and study the water. Usually I started with good intentions but the lure of the pool around the next corner was just too great and I ended up covering many kilometres in a day's fishing. Of course, at such speed I would spook several fish and no doubt miss many altogether. But on my first visit to the Hautapu, I was forced to abandon my usual tactics because of a Chinese dinner.

I was in Waiouru one November evening, intending to fish the river the next day. Casting an eye over the few eating establishments in town, I thought the Chinese takeaway joint looked the best of the limited options. However, on leaving the building I smashed my sandal-clad foot against the raised part of the old-style doorway. It hurt like hell, and I limped back to my motel convinced I had broken my big toe.

The next day the toe was black and blue and very sore. Getting it into a wading boot was going to be agony. I chose my largest pair, with room for stocking-foot waders, and was just able to ease in the swollen toe and lace the boot tight. Once in, the toe didn't seem quite so painful, and I certainly wasn't going to let a minor irritation like that ruin a precious day's fishing.

I drove down to where the stream flowed beside the main road and limped through the scrub to the water. It looked quite promising, being clean despite a silty bottom. It wasn't the most beautiful water I'd seen, but the reports of good fishing there spurred me on. A 40-knot head-wind was forecast, and the 6 weight outfit was looking like a good choice. I moved down the river and peered cautiously into the shallow run. It wasn't long before I spied some movement. A good-sized trout was quietly finning up the glide. I could see the opposite bank offered better cover, so I marked the fish's position for my return and quietly limped on. A promising start. There is nothing worse than trudging along a river and not seeing a trout all day.

Having spotted nothing more after about 2 km of painful progress, I was worrying I had bypassed the only fish in the river. A few casts here and there in the pocket water had produced nothing. My toe was really starting to hurt, so I sat down on the side of a hill well above a large pool. This seemed to be the start of a slower section, following a long stretch of faster water. As the toe throbbed and I wondered why I had bothered coming out, I spotted a movement at the head of the pool. A decent-sized trout was cruising along, obviously on a regular beat. With the toe needing more time to recover, I sat there and watched the trout for about fifteen minutes. This was contrary to my usual 'jump-in-and-thrash' tactic.

The brown was on a long, leisurely beat. It went slowly up for about 10 m, feeding all the way in water about half a metre deep. At the head of the pool, it turned and idled back down, feeding occasionally. You could see the white flash of its jaw as it intercepted a nymph. Its usual turning point was about halfway down the pool, where the inlet flow had dissipated and the current was very slow. But it didn't always turn here; it sometimes proceeded further, presumably when some more distant item of food took its fancy.

All this observation time allowed me to carefully work out the best approach. My plan of attack consisted of sneaking across the hill, down to the river and along the bank using the hillside as cover, to a spot 3 m from the trout's usual turning point. It took me ten minutes to quietly achieve this, after which I sat down and waited — my toe saying, 'Thank you'.

Several minutes passed, and I thought I had spooked my trout. With a good toe I would probably have given up and gone on to the next pool. However, I continued to sit, staring intently into the water through my Polaroids. All of a sudden, the fish swam into view, coming downstream. I waited for it to turn. Even when it did, I was scared that if I moved I would spook it, so I remained sitting as I tossed up a size 14 beadhead Hare'n'Copper'. It was a good first effort, and the nymph 'plipped' into the middle of the current tongue. The trout swam languidly over to inspect it. There was a flash, and I tightened. The startled 2 kg brown erupted from the quiet water. Solid sidestrain stopped its initial flight to its bolt hole somewhere at the head of the pool and got it down to the middle to fight on my terms. A few minutes and a photo later, it was back in the pool — and I had learned something more about trout-fishing.

It is quite surprising how you can look into a pool for a while and see nothing. But on the upper Hautapu, if you watch for at least ten minutes, you are just about guaranteed to see a trout in every pool. Their beats are all different. Some are very predictable and you could set your watch by the regularity of their lap around the pool. Others go AWOL for a while and you wonder what they're up to and where they've gone. Usually there's only one trout in each pool. The better pools, with cover from bankside vegetation, contain bigger trout, while the shallower, more open pools have smaller trout. The larger fish seem to have a more irregular cruising beat. Whether they have learned from previous experience that this is a safer practice is an interesting question. It is sometimes necessary to wait a long time for a big fish to repeat its circuit. Maybe animals moving on the hill above have spooked them in the past. For whatever reason, they just seem to head for cover for a while, but they are worth waiting for as there are not too many streams this size with so many large trout.

In the gorge, the fishing is a little easier. The flies to use in the faster water are beadhead Hare'n'Coppers or beadhead Caddis. The fur on these gives them more action, and the beadheads flash as the fly tumbles down the river, especially the newer, many-faceted varieties. The Caddis I use most is the Woolly Caddis, which imitates the green free-living caddis larvae. The pattern was first made famous by John Parsons, who used very little else on the trout around Taupo. I tend to follow his original dressing but have added the beadhead in recent times.

I recently saw another variation for when a heavier sinker fly is wanted. The idea is to load several small beadheads onto the shank of the hook. These give weight to the fly without your having to resort to environment-unfriendly lead. It also gives a realistic segmented look to the nymph. If you use one of these as your sinker and add a beadhead Hare'n'Copper as your tail fly, you should find a fish or two.

Below the gorge, there is no road access and only the railway track follows the river. If you know any friendly railway jigger drivers, you might do well. I once had some help from a track-worker when I was out early in the morning at the start of this section. Wandering down the river, I came to a pool just above a railway bridge. It was wide, with a narrow, slowish, rocky run at its head. There was manuka scrub surrounding the pool, so I carefully pushed a few branches aside to have a look for fish.

Immediately, I saw a huge trout sitting in about 30 cm of water over by the far bank. It was actively feeding, every now and then nipping out into the current and seizing a nymph. I could not cast to him from my side as the scrub was head-high, and if I pushed through the scrub to the river, he would be sure to spot me. I was considering my options when a jigger rolled over the bridge above. It stopped on the far side and a railway worker walked back along the track. He looked down and I hailed him.

'Can you see that fish opposite me?' I asked.

'Yeah, sure,' he replied. 'Are you going to catch it?'

'No,' I muttered under my breath, 'I'm going to throw rocks at it.' Then, 'Can you keep your eye on it while I move down a bit,' I asked politely.

'No problem,' he replied.

I exited the bush and re-entered a few metres further down, where I at least had room to get out a roll cast.

'Is it still there?' I asked my spotter.

'Yep,' came the taciturn reply.

Due to the dull, early-morning light, I couldn't see the fish from my new position, but I had marked its position from a clump of toitoi on the bank beside it. I cast well up the middle of the current, hopefully far enough away from my quarry not to spook it. As the nymph drifted by, the line hesitated. I lifted the rod, and it was on! But not for long. It tore off downriver, and I couldn't follow thanks to the thick scrub lining the banks. I lowered the rod to horizontal and leaned on it to try to turn the fish, but it wasn't long before my nymph came flying back to join me.

Commiserations came from above as my helper turned and walked back over the bridge. Oh well, at least I'd won round one. I always feel the real thrill in fly-fishing is the moment of the strike. That's when the adren-

Woolly Caddis

Hook: size 10–14 curved body
Tail: none, or small tuft of fur if desired
Body: mixture of green seal's fur (or possum or synthetic dubbing fur) with grey, black or khaki fur to give a variety of colours to match the natural. If weight is required, add lead wire under the fur.
Thorax: black seal's fur or substitute
Head: gold beadhead to suit hook size

aline flows. Once you've fooled the fish, it gets a bit mechanical. Sure, it can be exciting as you are dragged by a feisty trout several hundred metres down the river, but the real accomplishment is fooling the trout in the first place. Winning a long fight might give you some sense of satisfaction, but you have to be careful to make sure your catch survives. I'm never too upset if I lose a fish; it is better to have fished and lost than never to have fished at all.

The lower sections of the Hautapu do not offer the same quality of angling, so I recommend you concentrate on the middle and upper sections of this productive river. You may not catch many, but you will see some big'uns. If you take the time to study the water, you may latch onto a large cruising brown. But when you're celebrating your success that evening, just be careful coming out of the Chinese takeaway!

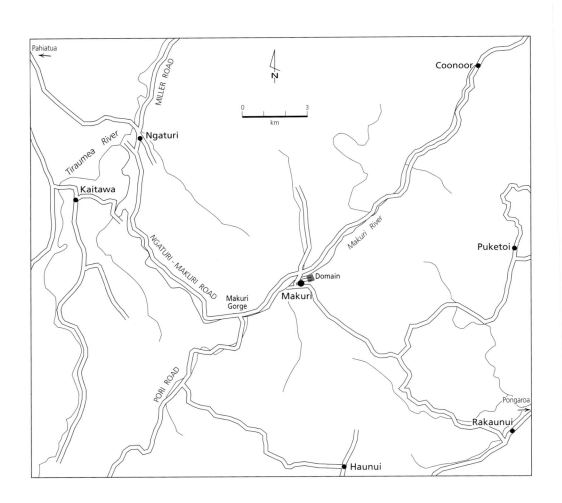

Makuri River
Fishing pocket water

DESCRIPTION AND DIRECTIONS

The Makuri River rises in the limestone country of the Waewaepa and Puketoi ranges, an area that feeds it a constant supply of clear, cold water. The result is a river with a chalk-stream nature. There are few such rivers in New Zealand, and they make for an interesting fishing experience.

In the upper reaches, the Makuri is more a creek than a river, winding through farmland until it reaches the small settlement of the same name. Below here, it changes nature completely as it tumbles through a rugged gorge, flanked by the beautiful native bush of the Makuri Scenic Reserve. Below the gorge, the river hides away in a channel some 30 m deep, worn out of the limestone over the millennia, and wends its way through farms until it joins the sluggish Tiraumea at Ngaturi. The fishing from the confluence up to the gorge is not particularly attractive.

Access to the river is from the Ngaturi–Makuri road, part of the road from Pahiatua to Pongaroa. The most popular section is around Makuri township, especially in the Makuri Domain. Here the river meanders between willowed banks, and access is easy. Wading is also easy, as the tails of the well-defined pools are mostly very shallow. Long, fine leaders are essential here as there is a lot of angling pressure. The trout average 1.5 kg, with the occasional bigger fish.

To fish the upper reaches, keep going straight ahead at the crossroads and the road follows the river for most of its length. Access is from any of the bridges or, with permission, through the adjoining farms. The river is quite small here, and early morning or late evening offer the best chance of success. When the sun is overhead, the petite pools are ruthlessly exposed and there is no cover. However, there have been reports of 3 kg fish being caught in these upper reaches, so they must hide somewhere during the day.

The gorge is for the fit angler, and not for the faint-hearted. The only easy access is via Pori Road, which turns off right about halfway through the gorge. The road crosses the river, where it is possible to make your way down at the front right-hand side of the bridge. It's quite a scramble, and worse coming back up, but if you make it you can pick your way downstream and fish an attractive wide stretch of rocky water about 50 m from the bridge. There always seems to be a fish or two in this run, as it is the first calm water after a long stretch of rapids. Below this, you're in for some hard work. 'Rugged' only begins to describe the terrain from here to the end of the gorge. There are many large boulders, and bushbashing is essential to get round them. Above the bridge, progress is a little easier once you get past the first big pool. There are some delightful short runs, and the river opens out in places, even allowing the occasional back cast.

As with most hard-to-fish stretches of any decent river, the results are worth the effort. The fish average 1.75 kg, with 3 kg being not uncommon. Landing them can be a problem, as it is quite an undertaking to follow a fish downstream in the gorge. However, the pleasure of fishing such wild water, enveloped by beautiful native bush, more than makes up for the odd lost fish.

TALES AND TECHNIQUES

The first impression you have on catching sight of the Makuri is . . . 'clear'. The next impression, as you set foot in it, is . . . 'cold'. This river differs greatly from many others in the Wellington region in that it remains cold even during the highest midsummer temperatures. While others are suffering from low flows, warm water and sluggish fish, the Makuri flows on cold and clear, even when drought conditions prevail. This ensures a flourishing trout population, and a river that, despite its intimate size, lives up to its reputation for large fish. Recent drift/dive surveys have counted a number of 3 kg trout.

The information from such surveys is always fascinating and often surprises local anglers, who tend to be convinced the fishing is 'nothing like the good old days'. I, too, have been a little sceptical about some of the trout counts I have read about for rivers in which I have done poorly. However, I recently discovered that a Wellington cousin-in-law of mine was the person in charge of many drift/dive surveys. When I tackled him about the 'head' counts, he assured me they were surprisingly accurate.

Apparently, once you have gained sufficient experience, it is relatively easy to count the trout as you swim through a pool. The trick is, like fielding in slips, to worry only about those fish to one side of you. Like a catch to slips, if the ball's on your inside hand, it's the other guy's problem. So the divers need to concentrate only on the trout on their inside hand, as far as the next diver. The only other points to record mentally are if a fish is a brown or a rainbow and which of the three size divisions it falls into. Where I would need a waterproof calculator to keep count, these survey scientists manage with just their heads.

Certainly the information produced by these surveys is invaluable — a great guide to where you have the best chance of catching a fish. It might even help with progress through the five stages of trout-fishing:

1) wanting to catch a trout
2) wanting to catch a lot of trout
3) wanting to catch a big trout
4) wanting to catch a lot of big trout
5) wanting to catch an 'uncatchable' trout.

We may never achieve stages 4 and 5, but the information gathered by Fish and Game in their drift/dive surveys definitely gives us a chance of advancing to the next level.

My experience of the Makuri is not at odds with the drift/dive results. It is a river that can produce a lot of fish, and the occasional big one as well. The most productive section is from just above the gorge, past the Makuri settlement. To get to it, turn right at the crossroads just after the top of the gorge. Makuri is only 1 km down this road, and on the way you cross a bridge over the river. You can fish from here down to the gorge, or up to the Makuri Domain, but there is a lot of angling pressure here because of the easy access compared with further downstream. An alternative is to turn hard left just over the bridge and follow a dirt road to the Makuri Domain, where you will find a golf course and an expansive building that houses the Makuri Club (which looks like the place to be on a Saturday night). From the golf course, there is easy access to the river and you can fish a long way up. The water is a nice size, with surprisingly deep pools that give plenty of cover. Fish can be spotted quite easily, so it is wise to approach cautiously. Long leaders and small flies are essential. The locals insist the best fly to use is a 'Lunkerbuster'. This was a new one on me, and sounds like an American pattern. I have not been able to find it in any of my own reference works but the pattern overleaf is close enough.

Lunkerbuster

Hook: size 12–16, standard round bend
Tail: few whisks of cream or ginger cock hackle, tied longer than usual
Body: black silk
Ribbing: fine copper wire
Thorax: grey fur, rough dubbed
Wing-case: cream or other light-coloured feather
Head: black silk

The last time I fished the upper river, this pattern worked very well, so it could be worth tying up a few before you head for the Makuri. But if this is too much trouble, call in at the local tackle shop — it has plenty.

Down in the gorge, the river is a very different beast — a cross between the Ruakituri and Waipunga rivers (see earlier chapters). It has the huge boulders of the Ruakituri to scramble over or bushbash around, plus the foliage-clutching progress up the edge of the Waipunga. Don't venture here without felt-soled boots and a wading stick. Below the Pori Road bridge, there are several big, deep pools interspersed with unfishable rapids, but it's doubtful if the fishing is worth the effort required to get there. There is better fishing above the bridge.

If you want an easier route to this water, enter the bush just above the one-way sign on the left-hand side. A relatively easy fifteen–minute walk through ponga and supplejack will bring you to a very attractive stretch of river. This saves you the clamber down the bank and the climb over boulders to get around the first big pool. In this stretch there are some pretty runs, some deep pools and a lot of pocket water. You may spot trout in the runs but otherwise you will be fishing blind.

The first time I fished the Makuri gorge, I had no idea what I was in for. Looking up from the Pori Road bridge, the river looked quite attractive. Being a regular Waipunga man, I found the bank-side bush posed no major problems. Once I had bushbashed around the first big pool, the going was reasonable and the pocket water looked good. The first drift through a pocket behind a large rock saw an enthusiastic take — by a trout not much larger than the nymph! But a couple of casts later, I was into something quite a bit larger. Downstream it fled, angler only just hanging on — all the way to the first large pool above the bridge. So much for all the effort to get up the river.

The 1.75 kg rainbow was eventually landed, and back I slogged. The thought of a repeat performance made me review my terminal tackle. I put on a 1.75 m braided leader and attached a metre of fluorocarbon tippet. This combination would be more abrasion-resistant, and the fluorocarbon was stronger for the same diameter than the nylon tippet I'd had on before. It is always a good idea anyway, when fishing the gorge, to increase your tippet strength by a kilo — say, from 2 kg up to 3 kg. Then your tail fly can be attached with 2.5 kg, which should be sufficient to handle most fish there. Another reason for a stronger tippet is that most of the good fish come from the pocket water. This means they usually take very strongly, often breaking thinner tippets.

I reckoned my new, stronger rig would allow me to put more pressure on a fish and keep it from heading so far downstream. Good theory! The next trout was a bit larger and took off like a torpedo at full throttle. It was down to the big pool once more, where I landed a 2 kg fish before hauling myself back upriver to cast again.

It was obvious the fish were all lying in the pocket water, so it was a matter of concentrating on thoroughly fishing all such spots. I carried on

Fishing pocket water.

up the gorge trying every pocket. About 1.5 km from the bridge, there was a long narrow stretch filled with large boulders, which obscured much of the water as it flowed around and under them. There were no fish-holding pockets for as far as I could see, and I didn't fancy the long clamber to reach the next fishable stretch. It had already taken me four hours to get this far, and the four trout I had landed were a good result for my first time on the river. The early discovery that the fish were lying in the pockets had been the key to the day's success.

Pocket water can be described as any spot where there is some hesitation in the downstream rush of fast water. The slowing of the flow can be caused by a boulder, partly submerged rock, log or other obstruction. Good-sized trout lie here because the obstruction gives them shelter from the swift current, while the choppy surface gives them protection from predators. In addition, the river brings down a constant stream of food right past their noses. Pocket-dwelling fish have little time to assess the food racing past and use a 'dash-and-grab' approach. They nick out into the current, grab the morsel and race back to the protection of the pocket, where they decide whether to ingest the seized item. This food-

Makuri Gorge.

gathering technique makes for some violent takes, which is why a strong tippet is needed. The heavier trace is no deterrent, as a trout doesn't have time to notice it.

It is essential to fish close to a pocket, as you need to be able to steer your nymph around the pocket-forming obstruction and into the slacker water behind. This gives the fish a chance to intercept the fly before the fast water carries it away. The pocket should be approached from behind and to one side. A short cast should be made above the pocket and the rod raised to lift most of the line off the water. It pays not to lift the rod too high, though, as some upward motion is needed for the strike, unless you are a proficient 'line-hand' striker. Steer the fly around the obstruction and along the edge of the pocket. Retrieve excess line as the fly comes towards you, as you need to be in direct contact when it swings into the pocket. When the indicator dips, strike by lifting the rod and also pulling with your line hand to straighten the leader in the confused current.

A high-floating indicator is usually needed in the gorge, as anything else tends to be pulled under by the turbulent water. Yarn-type indicators do not work well, as they require the flick of false-casting to dry them out

between drifts. As very often there is not the room to false-cast, the foam types are a better choice. I use the snap-on ones that can be adjusted up and down the leader to suit the depth of the water being fished. They come in four sizes and two colours, so are flexible in terms of water and light conditions.

The flies that suit pocket fishing are normally bigger than those you would use on more gentle waters. My first choice is a weighted size 10 beadhead Hare'n'Copper, tied to be especially bushy — the rougher look-ing, the better. Second choice is a size 8 Stonefly, brown or green depend-ing on which type is most prevalent on the river. Other recommended nymphs include the Zug Bug, Bitch Creek and Woolly Worm. Generally, any large nymph with material that waves around as it tumbles down in the current will do fine. You are trying to imitate a nymph that has been dislodged from its hold on the rock above and is being tossed this way and that by the confused waters.

Pocket fishing is great fun and doesn't need as much skill as fishing to educated trout in quieter water. This was proven when I took a French col-league up the gorge a few years ago. He had never fly-fished before so had no idea even how to cast a line. However, he was a keen bait fisherman in the small trout streams around Lyon. It took only ten minutes to teach him how to flick a line from downstream up to the pocket a maximum of 3 m away. From his long fishing experience, I assumed he would know where the fish lay. Providing he could get the fly up to the pocket, I figured he would have a good chance of catching a trout. So it proved. Jean was very adept at guiding the nymph through the pockets, as that was exactly what he did fishing worms on a threadline outfit back home. He lost a few trout but ended up with two beautifully speckled browns at the end of the morning. The biggest weighed 1.5 kg. This was, he informed me on the way home, five times heavier than the biggest trout he had ever caught in his home waters.

When we catch a 1.5 kg fish, most of us throw it back and go looking for a 'decent-sized' one. Sometimes we just don't appreciate what we have in this trout-fishing paradise, and it takes the viewpoint of a visitor to bring this home to us. If the Makuri River were in Lyon, it would probably be fished out in short order. Here it remains one of the Wellington area's best-kept secrets.

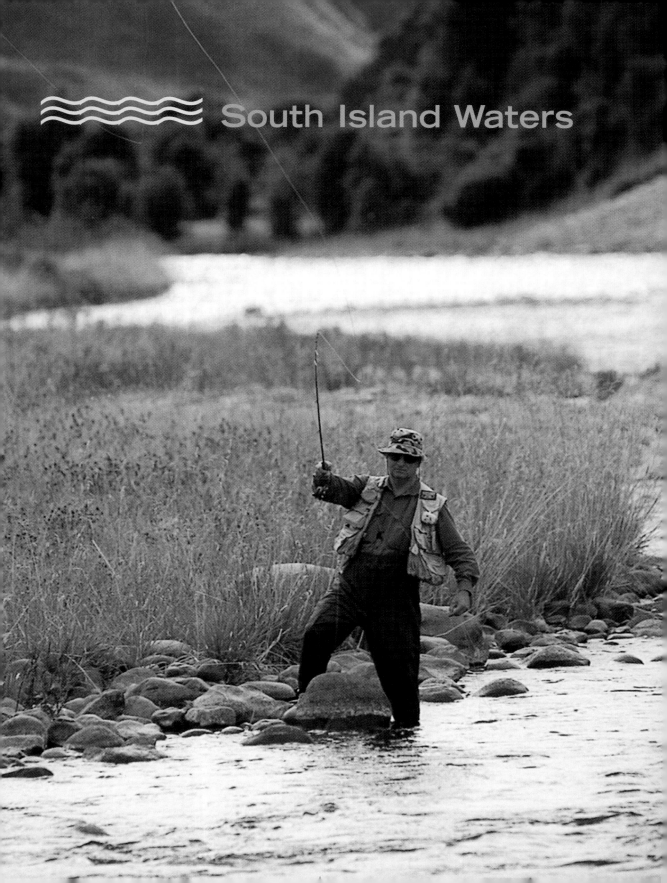

South Island Waters

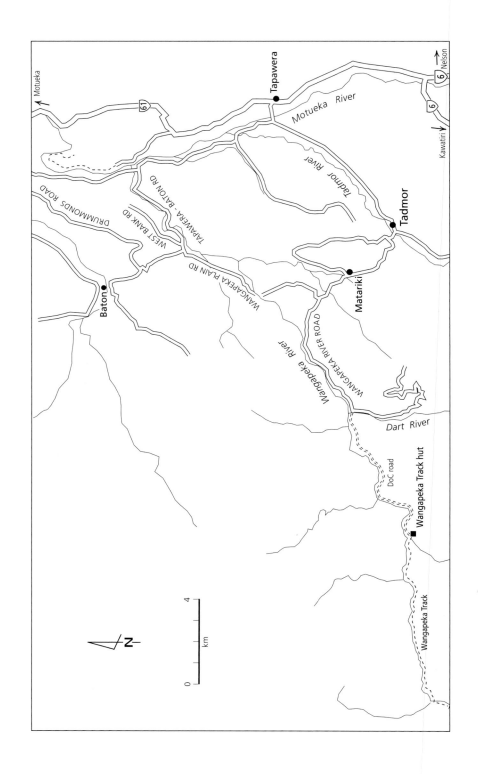

Wangapeka River
Spotting trout

DESCRIPTION AND DIRECTIONS

The depths of the Kahurangi National Park in northwest Nelson are the source of the beautiful Wangapeka River. This rises on the slopes of Mt Patriarch, so steep and mountainous it has been used by climbers training for assaults on Mt Everest. The upper river is easily accessed from the Wangapeka Track, which follows it for over 15 km. The track is well formed, and winds through dense red and silver beech forest. It is often above the river, making it necessary to push down through the trees and ferns to get to the water.

The deep, turquoise-green pools look as if they are bound to hold trout — and they do, but mainly old and wily browns that have survived the onslaught of passing trampers. The average weight is 2 kg, though 5 kg fish are not uncommon. They do not get that big by being easy to catch though, so stealth is essential. But the cautious approach should not include the use of ultralight leaders. Any leader under 2 kg will not last long, thanks to the legendary power of the Wangapeka trout. Be ready for a charge downstream over and around huge boulders to follow your big fish.

Make sure, too, that you take only a photo of your trophy, as this is a delicately balanced fishery thanks to a huge flood in early 1998 that killed half of the resident fish. Most of the damage from that '100-year' event can be seen in the middle reaches, along the road leading to the start of the track. The road is well signposted from Tapawera and first meets the river about 10 km from the road end. There are two designated 'anglers' access' points, and it is possible to do a day's fishing there and walk back to your car along the road.

From the Dart River confluence down, the water has a slightly brown colour from the dark, peat-coloured inflow from that tributary. Above the confluence are 6 km of runs, riffles and pools up to the end of the park access road and the start of the track. This is beautiful water, with browns feeding freely in the shallows of the bubbly runs. Fish numbers can be variable but careful observation will ensure enough to keep most anglers happy.

The lower reaches are accessed from the road on the right just over the Motueka River bridge near Tapawera. This road follows the Motueka for some way before it veers left and meets the Wangapeka just up from the confluence with the Motueka. There are several designated 'anglers' access' points along the road, and again it is easy to fish from one to the next and stroll back down the road. The river here is quite wide but relatively shallow, so it can be crossed easily in normal flows. The fish tend to be smaller than in the upper reaches but give a good account of themselves. They average around 1.25 kg, with good numbers of larger trout, although these usually appear only at dawn and dusk, as they tend to feed in the glides and runs rather than the pools.

The lack of cover in the shallow water means the trout do not feel secure if there is light on the water. Poor light for the angler means fish are hard to spot, and prospecting techniques are required. As there is a lot of water to cover, it is essential to fish slowly and carefully, or fish will be missed. During the day, it is often also necessary to fish 'blind', as the smaller ones are difficult to see in the boisterous water. The lower reaches are nowhere near as scenic as the upper, so for those wanting beauty *and* the beast, the longer trek to the upper section is well worthwhile.

TALES AND TECHNIQUES

The upper reaches of the Wangapeka are an example of a true New Zealand wilderness river. Fortunately for anglers, the beauty of the area has resulted in a well-formed tramping track alongside. This makes it easy to walk beside the river, stopping off to fish at likely looking spots, of which there are plenty. The best time to be on the river is early or late, as the bigger fish tend to hide in the depths of the huge pools during the day. Sometimes they can be tempted to come up for a big Stonefly, and I have even seen the odd one rise to the surface for a Cicada in the middle of a hot summer's day. Generally, though, they are active early on and then lie 'doggo' for the remaining daylight hours, moving into the shallows to feed only when the light has begun to fade. This makes life a bit difficult for the daytime angler, as it is a long drive from civilisation to the upper reaches of the Wangapeka. Unless you feel like rising well before dawn or walking home in darkness, the only option for giving yourself a decent chance at the big fish is to stay in one of the park huts.

The pristine water of the Wangapeka.

A trout lying at the bottom of a deep pool, is there because it feels secure and will rarely come up to take a fly. It may feed if something tempting is drifted along the bottom of the pool, but otherwise the trout remain in the security of the deep water until the light lessens and they feel it is safe to move to shallower water. On many rivers, they might feed in the security of the riffles, but the upper Wangapeka is one of those rivers that can be described as having a 'classical' structure. Such rivers have cavernous deep pools fed by turbulent rapids at the head and a shallow tail leading to the next rapid. There are few riffly stretches as the river consists of a long series of these classic pools. Spotting fish in the clear pools is relatively easy, but getting down to their level is not. It is necessary to resort to long leaders and heavy flies. However, when fishing such a beautiful wilderness river, you don't feel much like employing 'Tongariro' techniques.

The first time I fished the upper Wangapeka, I wasn't expecting to use such tactics and set off with my 6 weight, four-piece rod in my backpack. My wife, Sue, came along for the walk, and we hiked for an hour or so before I started to examine the water. Peering through the beech trees, I saw a nice rocky run that looked very 'fishy'. I asked Sue to stay on the track where she could look down into the water. It is really handy, on clear South Island rivers, to have a spotter. The best way to operate is in pairs, with partners fishing and spotting by turn. It is a lot easier to see trout from above the river than down next to it. The spotter can give directions, enabling the angler to keep well back from the fish and avoid getting too close trying to see where it is lying and how it is feeding. Having someone feeding you a running commentary on the movements of the fish gives you a distinct advantage. Although Sue does not fish, I was hoping she could undertake spotting duties for a while.

I slithered down the bank and crossed the river at the tail of the run. As is usual with clear rivers, it was deeper than it looked and a trifle cold around the nether regions. Regaining the far bank, I tackled up and advanced to the water's edge.

'Can you see anything?' I asked my spotter.

'Not yet,' came the reply.

'Well, go up a bit further but make sure you stay back in the trees.'

'Yeah, yeah,' came the reply, 'I'm not stupid, you know.'

Not wanting to lose her services so early, I choked back my rejoinder.

'I can see one!' came the cry a couple of minutes later. 'Just above that light-coloured rock up there.'

'How far out is it lying?' I asked.

'About 2 metres from the bank,' Sue replied.

'Is it moving about much?'

Sue studied the water for a minute. 'No, it seems to be just sitting there.'

I carefully walked up to about 10 m below the indicated rock and stripped out some line.

'Still there?' I asked.

'Yep, it hasn't moved.'

I made a cast deliberately short of the indicated position just to get a feel for the distance.

'That was too far below it,' came the immediate response. I didn't bother to field that one but recast, this time a metre above the light rock and half a metre to one side.

'That was right over its nose,' Sue informed me.

'Did it move at all?'

'Nope.'

I cast again, this time closer to the indicated position. No response. Twenty casts later, and still no response, I advanced to where I could see the target. Peering into the water, I identified the problem.

'You know what that is?' I asked the spotter.

'What?'

'It's a "rock fish",' I informed her.

'What's a . . . oh, I see. Well, how am I supposed to know what's a fish and what's a rock?' Sue asked. 'I'll go and read my book and you can find them yourself.'

That was it for trout-spotting for the day. But I had to admit the rock did look very fishy, even through my Polaroids. It was the right length, and the flow patterns around it gave the impression of movement. The only giveaway was that on a bright sunny day there was no fish-shaped shadow on the riverbed.

Spotting trout is an inexact science at the best of times. When conditions are on your side, it is easy to see fish, especially in clear, placid waters. But such trout will tend to be cautious, as they are well aware of how visible they are. In rougher, more turbulent water, trout are much harder to see. It pays to look for movement first, as this is the most reliable indicator. (Rocks do not tend to move much.) Or you may see just a flash of colour, particularly from rainbows or golden-sided browns. The white flash of a jaw opening is another good pointer, especially as it indicates a feeding trout. If a fish is not moving much, look for a shadow on the side away from the sun. Because it will be lying clear of the bottom, its shadow will be more distinct than that of an embedded rock. And rock shadows do not move, so a bit of patient observation will usually determine if the likely object is worth a cast. The best idea is to mark its position against a distinctive rock, stone or other natural feature. Keep checking its position against this, and if it doesn't move in relation to the marker, it is either unlikely to be a trout or is asleep and not feeding.

When conditions become difficult, as on overcast days, expert spotters come into their own. Unfortunately I am not of this elite breed. I can peer into a pool for several minutes before someone like my Napier mate

Spotting by colour.

Frank comes along and immediately points out a good fish I haven't seen. I can then stare, for another minute or so, right at the indicated spot before a vague troutlike shape materialises against the riverbed. I have no idea how these guys do it. When you ask them, they say they're examining the water for something that doesn't look quite right. It may be a suggestion of movement, a hint of a shadow, a variation in colour or a shape that suggests a fish. These are the indicators an expert spotter uses to distinguish a trout from a likely-looking stone or clump of weed. Whatever the level of your spotting skills, they need to be honed. Regularly. There is no doubt that the more you look for fish, the easier it becomes to register their presence. It may not be possible for all of us to be experts, but we can, with practice, become reasonably proficient.

The next trout spotted on that day was a few hundred metres further

Spotting by shape.

up the track. The river was out of sight as the track had veered away and we were walking through some attractive bush. I noticed a cairn of rocks piled up at the start of a rough side path. Acting on a hunch, I detoured down the path and a few minutes later emerged by a glorious pool. The water tumbled down steep rapids, smashed into a large cliff on the far side, then surged along the cliff face, widening into a large, deep, aquamarine pool.

As I peered through the trees, I immediately saw a big fish lying very deep in the heart of the pool. Presumably a previous angler had built the cairn to remind them where the fish was on their way back. I pushed through the trees down to the tail of the pool and crept out onto the bank. I figured the fish was lying at least 3 m deep, so changed my tippet nylon for a longer one of 2 m to go with my 3 m leader. I added a small indicator to the top of the leader, then dug out a Tongariro 'bomb' as a sinker fly to get my size 14 Pheasant Tail down to the trout's level. I tied on the sinker with its attendant fly and tossed the whole lot downstream into the rapids at the pool tail.

There was no way the poor little 6 weight was going to keep 5 m of leader and a heavy nymph airborne. Allowing the leader to straighten, I hauled on the line to break the surface tension, then tossed the whole caboodle into the centre current well above the trout. The line drifted down nicely but I wasn't sure if I should concentrate on the trout or the indicator. It was rather unusual to be able to see a fish at such depth so clearly. I saw the trout move, and then looked at the indicator. After what seemed a long time, it moved. I struck hard to straighten the long leader, and there was a satisfying jerk as the fly bit home. But elation was brief. I had been too slow with the take, and a few seconds later the trout threw the hook. If only I had struck when I had seen the trout move! However, the experience had been a good lesson in how long it takes an indicator, positioned 5 m from the fly, to register the take. It was only the clarity of the water that had enabled me to see a fish, 3 m down, move to the fly. A good trout had been lost, but another piece had been fitted into the fishing-knowledge jigsaw.

Further up the river, there were more fish to be seen — not many, but easily enough to fill the remaining three hours' fishing time. All were lying deep in the huge pools, and it was hard work getting a fly down to them. They may have been where they were because they had sought a stable refuge after the flood, but I would like to have been there at dusk, when I suspect they would have moved up to feed in the eye of the pool. Unfortunately that was not to be, and soon it was time to start back down the track. It had been a delightful day — even if I had lost the services of one spotter.

In the Wangapeka's peat-coloured middle reaches, spotting is more difficult. It is necessary to fish the pools blind, as trout cannot be seen in the depths. However, there are more secondary runs and riffles below the Dart confluence, and trout can be spotted there when they are feeding in the shallows. They tend to do this most often when the light is low, but as there are some good riffles not far from the road it is possible to fish through the evening feeding time. You can wander down the river and fish your way back up, timing your arrival for the moment when the sun falls below the high mountains.

Similar tactics work well on the lower river, near the confluence with the Motueka River. The trout here also seem to prefer the deep pools during the day and venture out into the shallows only when the sun is off the water. As the road follows the river for much of this section, again it is possible to fish near your car. This means you can safely negotiate your way back to the road and don't have to stumble through scrub or bush in failing light. There is some very good evening fishing water near the last 'anglers' access', not far up the road from the bridge. The river has an open, braided nature on the road side, and you fish towards the beech forest lining the far bank. It is a delightful spot to be in as the sun sinks behind the mountains of the Kahurangi National Park — particularly when the snout of a large brown breaks through the silvery surface.

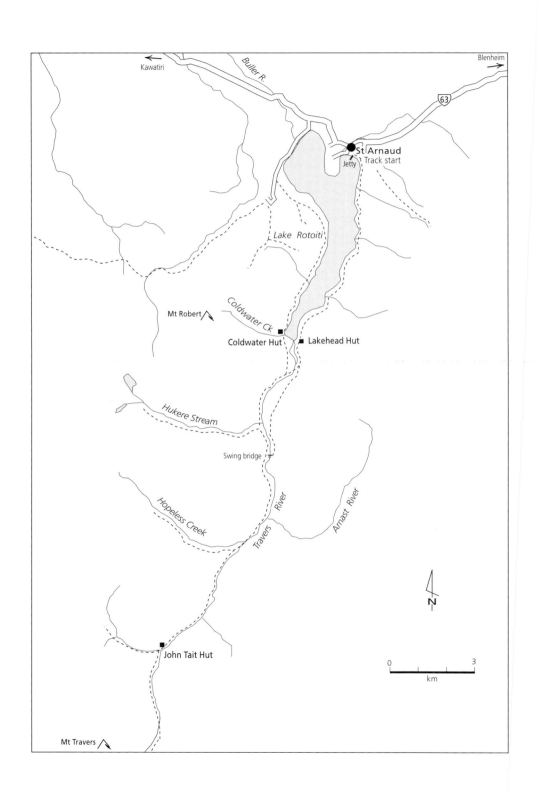

Travers River
Casting techniques

DESCRIPTION AND DIRECTIONS

The Travers River rises in the heart of the St Arnaud Range in the Nelson Lakes area. It flows for about 15 km from the foothills of Mt Travers through pristine beech forest to Lake Rotoiti. It enters the lake at the top end, while the mighty Buller River starts its long journey at the other end.

Access to the Travers is via a tramping track around the lake. This starts at the pleasant hamlet of St Arnaud, and it is a three-hour walk to the mouth of the river. For a day-fisher, it pays to take the water taxi, which, for a modest fee, saves you the walk and allows you to get on with fishing. The taxi goes to either the Lakehead Hut jetty or the Coldwater Hut.

The mouth of the river is right next to the Coldwater Hut, and it's worth exploring the waters just up from the lake, as some big trout frequent the lower 100 m of the river. Staying overnight at the hut gives you the opportunity to pick up a good fish in the early morning or on a dry fly at night. It is also here that Coldwater Creek enters the Travers River. There is the odd fish up this stream but it is probably worth fishing only in the middle of summer. Be warned: the creek is freezing cold — even by South Island standards.

Apart from around the mouth, the lower Travers is not of much interest except early or late in the season. The bottom consists mainly of gravel, and the river lacks the depth or obstructions that give trout cover, a situation made worse by a lack of trees for several hundred metres. Better water is to be found about 30 minutes' walk up from the lake. You will come to a slip across the track. Moving through the paddocks on the left brings you to two of the best pools on the river. The first is a long, deep, green pool that reflects the tall beech trees on the far bank. A careful approach is essential, as angling pressure has made the trout there very wary. Two hundred metres further up the river there is a delightful pool that hugs the far bank. It is longer but shallower than the first, and usually harbours four or five trout that are superselective and ignore any fly that doesn't seem 'right'.

For the next few kilometres, up to the swing bridge, there are a number of smaller pools and runs that may reveal a trout to the observant angler. The river is somewhat braided, thanks to the flood-prone nature of the Travers. Fish tend to lie in the shallows, and most fishing is to visible trout. The two long pools by the swing bridge often contain a few large trout, but they get everything thrown at them by passing trampers. Above the swing bridge, the river splits in two. As long as it isn't low, this is a profitable stretch, as it is fished less than the waters nearer the lake. It is about two hours' walk into this area, so not too many day anglers get far up this section of water. To reach the more secluded pools it is necessary to push through the bush, but the reward is fish that are not quite as fussy as those further down. The average weight is around 1.5 kg, with an occasional 3 kg fish to be seen.

The Travers Valley.

Further up the valley, the river is smaller and harder to get to — more the province of adventurous angling trampers. But that still leaves more than 8 km of genuine wilderness river, which should be more than enough for most anglers to fish in a day.

TALES AND TECHNIQUES

The Travers is a typical Nelson area river. Although it is not easy to get to, it still receives the heavy angling pressure common to most rivers in the region. It is the possibility of a big fish that draws anglers from far and wide to Nelson area waters. This is also why these rivers can be more renowned overseas than in New Zealand. If you stay at a hotel in the area, you are likely to hear American accents in the dining room and observe a professional guide's 4WD pulling up at a 'civilised' hour in the morning. In will pile two or three visiting anglers and off they'll go to try for their 'trophy'. Most of these anglers are competent and well directed by their local 'coach'. The result of this combination of skills is some very educated fish.

Recent studies by a Nelson research centre have shown that after a trout has been caught it won't feed again for quite some time — several days in some cases. And when it does, it will be even more discerning about what food it accepts. If there is anything suspect, a refusal is guaranteed. It isn't so much that the fish are spooky, more that they're fussy. If your presentation is reasonable, you can cast over a fish 50 times with every fly you have and it will steadfastly ignore your offerings while continuing to feed on the real stuff. Whether it recognises your fly is artificial, or your drift isn't right, or there's a smidgen of drag, or the leader is too shiny — whatever the reason, the fish won't take. I have even heard the local guides no longer waste time on such picky trout. If a fish doesn't take after a few casts, they advise their client to move on to the next, in the hope it will prove more naïve.

All this can result in some very frustrated anglers. Of course, we do have the choice of not fishing such waters and heading off to some more remote, less well-known river, but that would be to deny ourselves some of the best fishing terrain in the world. There are not too many places where you can watch a 3 kg trout feeding away in cold, crystal-clear water, so why should we forego that pleasure just because the fish is hard to fool? No, what we have to do is somehow develop a more successful approach than the anglers before us. This doesn't necessarily mean you have to be a better fisherman. It may simply entail getting up earlier or staying later, when the fish are feeding more freely. Or perhaps studying the prevalent insect life more closely than the angler who sticks with the same fly all day.

One simple solution is to fish the more difficult spots. The easiest way to do this is to walk further up the river than the average angler before you start. It is noticeable all around New Zealand that most angling activity along a river takes place within one hour's walk of the nearest road access point. What begins as a heavy concentration of footprints will gradually thin out as you advance upriver. That said, there is no guarantee these days that when you have slogged in for four hours you won't hear the woofing noise of a helicopter setting down at the pool just round the corner.

Another easy solution is to look for places other anglers would consider too much like hard work to reach. These are generally the least accessible spots. To get to them might involve a deep wade, a scramble up a cliff or, more commonly, a bushbash. But that is where the good keen man can gain an advantage over his well-heeled competitor. There is almost always a pool or two that can be accessed only through the bush. By shoving your way through the dense foliage, you can find yourself peering down at a trout that is not quite as educated as those elsewhere in the river. Then you have a better than even chance.

Once you get into such an inhospitable spot, of course, another reason why other anglers give it such a wide berth will become obvious. There is no room to cast! Then you have to be proficient at casting from difficult positions. This may require practice and the learning of a few new techniques. Some casts to use in such situations are:

The roll cast: the most useful cast in difficult positions. It is normally used where there is no chance of a back cast. Draw the rod slowly towards you, using the friction of the water on the line to load it up. When the rod reaches two o'clock, snap it forward, propelling the line in a roll towards the river. Initially, you are unlikely to achieve much distance and will tend to splash the line down heavily on the water. It doesn't take much practice to achieve reasonable distance, but a gentle landing — necessary when fishing to a visible trout — takes a bit more work. The roll cast is also great for giving mend to your fly line before it hits the water (i.e. aerial mending).

The side cast: used where there is insufficient overhead clearance for a roll cast. The plane of the cast is horizontal rather than vertical — like a baseball swing instead of a golf swing. It is most helpful under overhanging branches or foliage — a favourite trout location. Concentrate on keeping the fly low, as there is a tendency to forget the fly line must turn over before it lands. If you don't have a tight loop, you will see your fly irretrievably entangled in an overhanging branch. Evidence of previous failures is usually visible, dangling above fishy-looking spots on popular rivers.

The from-the-current cast: one of the best casts for close situations. The strength of the current is used to load the rod before the forward cast is

The side cast.

made. Allow the line to drift completely past and swing around down-stream until it is fully straightened by the current. With your line hand, pull some line in to break the surface tension and then drive your rod hand forward to fling the line upstream. The technique can be used on either the forehand or the backhand, depending on which side of the river you find yourself. If your backhand is weak, you can try to become a little ambidextrous and make a forehand cast with your non-natural hand.

This cast is also ideal when you are using heavy nymphs, as it avoids the danger those 'bombs' pose as they drop on the back cast and come

The 'from the current' cast.

forward at earlobe height. It is easy to keep the low-flying nymph well away from your person by bringing the rod through at 45 degrees. Again, it takes some practice to get the nymph to land gently in delicate situations, but by aiming the cast upwards, and finishing with the rod higher than normal, it is possible to achieve a gentle drop.

The steeple cast: used where there is no possibility of a back cast due to foliage behind. Throw the line upwards rather than backwards, then drive it forward. It is hard to get a gentle landing, and usually a roll cast is a better option unless greater distance is needed. The best I ever saw was by an old guy fishing below the main highway bridge on the Tongariro. He had an ancient, 4 m long, two-handed rod and was fishing with his back to a 5 m high bank. He flung the big rod straight up towards the sky, paused for a long moment while the line straightened, then hurled the whole lot forward across the river. When the fly landed just short of the far bank, I was rather impressed, but fishing all day with such a heavy rod would call for more time in the gym!

The backward cast: useful where there is a narrow gap in the foliage behind. Turn round and make a normal forward cast into the gap, then use your back cast as your cast up the river. The only trick is to ease off on your final back cast so you get a delicate presentation as the line comes forward. Again, with practice, considerable accuracy can be achieved with this backward delivery. It is better into the wind than a roll cast as more distance can be obtained.

The bow-and-arrow cast: great for tight situations but requires good coordination. Grab the fly between thumb and forefinger and pull out a metre of fly line. Hold the rod firmly in whatever position the foliage allows and draw away the hand holding the fly. This loads the rod, so when you release the fly, the rod snaps forward and throws the fly towards the water. It is a matter of getting the timing right: release too soon, and the fly goes nowhere; release too late, and the hook is driven into a tender appendage. Accordingly, it pays to use this cast only when all other options have been ruled out.

The steeple cast.

The change-of-direction cast: useful where the back cast straight behind is impossible. In fact, many anglers use it automatically without realising they are doing so. Back-cast in whichever direction you have room, then pivot to bring the rod forward in the direction of the fish. Watch the path of the fly coming forward because halfway through the cast it will start to track on the final trajectory and can get caught up on the trouble behind even though you have back-cast well away from it.

The best use of this cast is to reduce your false- or aerial-casting. If you cast onto dead water, you can lift the line from it, change direction and cast towards the intended landing area. This ensures your fly spends more time in the water than in the air. Surprisingly enough, if your fly spends more time in the water, you will catch more fish.

One wonders if some anglers appreciate this fact. I remember standing on the bridge over the Tongariro many years ago watching an angler fishing the pool below.

'That guy's pretty good,' remarked my French colleague.

'Yeah, he can certainly cast a line,' I agreed, watching the angler false-cast six or seven times before delivering the fly. 'However, unless he's after flying fish, he won't catch a lot.'

I explained that although he was a superb caster, he spent too much time false-casting to be very successful. We carried on to the Hydro Pool and stood watching an angler fishing towards us from the other side of the river.

'Now there's a good fisherman,' I indicated. 'See how he lifts the line in one motion from the river and makes only one false cast? He's using a change-of-direction cast. He'll catch a lot more fish than the other guy because his fly is in the water three times as much.'

The angler across the river looked up, raised his cap and doffed it in my direction.

'Gee, thanks, Gillies,' he said.

I was startled, not realising our voices had carried so far. I looked more closely at the now bareheaded angler.

'Bloody Harris!' I replied. ' If I had known it was you, I would have told him you were the worst I had seen!'

'Too late now, Gillies, you've dropped the ball again.'

The angler had turned out to be my old cricket mate Austin Harris, one of the best casters I have ever seen. I had certainly picked the right man to point out to my French visitor. So we trooped back over to join Austin on the open side of the pool, where my Frenchman received some expert tuition. Austin concentrated on the from-the-current cast, as he considers this the quickest way to get a beginner fly-fishing.

I put the cast to good use myself on the Travers on one visit in March. I had walked for about one-and-a-half hours to get to less popular water. I chose a heavily bushed area on the true left bank to use my left-handed advantage. A few minutes' scramble brought me to the river's edge. Peering into the shaded water, I discerned the shape of a good trout lying a metre out from the bank and a metre deep. The foliage would allow me only a short from-the-current-cast, so I let out a few metres of line into the current. When the line straightened, I flicked the size 14 Pheasant Tail forward. It plipped in a metre above and to the side of the trout. The fish finned over to inspect the tasty morsel. A white flash, and I tightened. The trout put up a strong fight but it was not too long before a 2.5 kg rainbow was safely in the net.

Peering through heavy bush.

The next fish was in just as difficult a spot, about 100 m further up the river. I had scrambled through bush down a bank to get to the water's edge after spotting it from the track above. Emerging from the under-growth, I tried to relocate it. After a minute or so, I saw it move out into the current to intercept an item of food. To get the right drift my only option was a reverse roll cast. The first effort was pathetic, but fortunately it landed harmlessly in the faster water. The next was better, just to the edge of the centre riffle. I struck to the dip of the indicator and the fight was on. The fish tore off downstream and I had no option but to jump into the waist-deep water and follow as far as the next pool. Now I was able to put some pressure on the fish and finally another 2.5 kg brown came to the net.

This success showed that on heavily fished rivers like the Travers, expertise in casting from difficult spots can see you score a fish or two. The trout you encounter from your hard-won bankside possie are likely to be both bigger and less cautious than those lying exposed in an open pool. If you have been diligent with your casting practice in the off-season, you will have a good chance of picking up a trout to remember in the stunning Travers Valley.

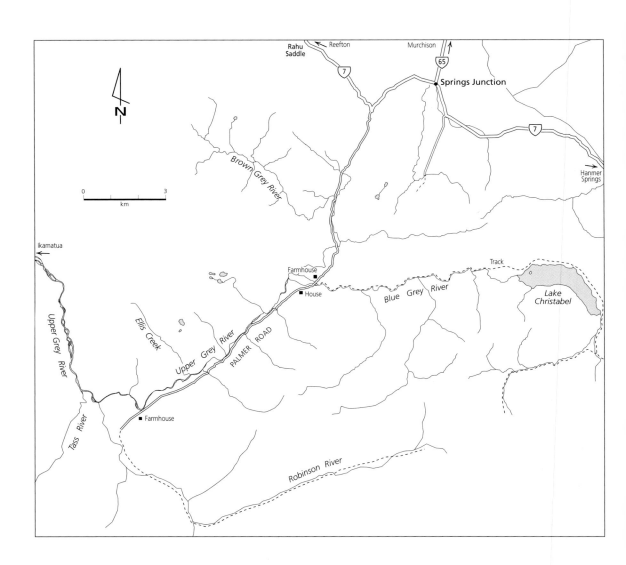

Blue Grey River
Adjusting to varying depths of water

DESCRIPTION AND DIRECTIONS

The Blue Grey starts its life at Lake Christabel in the hills behind Springs Junction, at the northern end of the Lewis Pass. The river flows very swiftly from the lake, down to where it joins the Brown Grey River. This smaller tributary may hold fish during the spawning season but is generally too shallow to afford the cover needed by mature trout. Being lake-fed, the Blue Grey River is much larger, so there is plenty of holding water for trout from the lake down.

Fishing spots are hard to find in the headwaters, however, as the river there consists of a narrow gully with a large volume of water pouring through. It is necessary to hike up the track to the lake and peer through the trees to see if you can spot any pockets where the river momentarily slows its headlong charge. Only a few such pools are to be found in the hour or so's walk to the lake, and they are easy to miss. They are also short and fast, so it is necessary to fish the quieter water at the edges. If you manage to hook a fish, your problems will have only begun, as it will be off downstream as soon as it feels the steel.

The better fishing water is found downstream from the bridge at the farm on Palmer Road, near the start of the track to the lake. The river meanders its way through farmland for a kilometre or so down to the Brown Grey confluence. From here, it is officially named the Upper Grey River, but most locals refer to it as the Blue Grey as far down as the Robinson confluence. This may be as much to do with the colour of the water as for any other reason.

On the corner just below the Brown Grey junction is a deep pool that always harbours some big browns. However, it is fished regularly by the locals so the fish are wary, even by South Island standards. Further down, the river enters bush. So long as the water level is normal, you can edge your way up either bank with only the occasional bit of bushbashing. There are some classic pools, with riffly water in between. Most of the fish are to be found lying at the edges of the secondary flows.

Palmer Road continues to follow the river for several kilometres, finishing at a farm gate marked 'Private Property'. It is necessary to call in at the farmhouse here to obtain permission to pass through the farm. From the end of the farm road, it is a short walk to the Robinson confluence, where the Grey River proper can be said to start. It is 13 km through some rugged country down to the next access.

This is one of the most beautiful rivers in New Zealand, crystal-clear water flowing over clean stones and big boulders. The fish are all browns and average around 1.75 kg with an occasional 4 kg fish to be seen.

The stretch above the Robinson confluence offers delightful fishing in a beech-flanked gorge. It is possible to work right through the gorge up to the start of the farm. Although the flow is strong, there are plenty of obstructions offering shelter to the hardy browns. There are riffles, runs, deep pools and many of the secondary flows the fish prefer. From the junction up is as good as South Island fishing gets — strong fish in clear water, with beech forest for a backdrop. Let's hope there are still a few years left of unrestricted access.

TALES AND TECHNIQUES

A grey smudge. No, this is not some deadly new fly, or a cross between a Smurf and a midge. It is what guide Tony Busch calls a brown trout when spotted in the Blue Grey River — a grey smudge against a blue-grey bottom. Of course, when the sun is out and the fish are lying shallow, they have the golden-brown look of trout in other rivers. But when a Blue Grey brown is out in its pool, that's what you look for — a grey smudge.

Just because Blue Grey trout are easy to spot does not mean they are easy to catch, as the Upper Grey is coming under increasing angling pressure. The local guides obviously find it a suitable river on which to give their clients the real Kiwi outdoor experience without the cost of a helicopter or the inconvenience of tramping in. One suspects the time cannot be far off when the local farmer will close off access in a deal with a professional guide, as is happening along many North Island rivers. In the meantime, Farmer Brian is very free with his access permission, so long as you don't look like the type who will nick tools out of the tractor shed on the way out. (Yes, he has had a few visiting anglers do just that.)

There are a lot more anglers than a few years ago, and the days of having the river to yourself are long gone. This means spooky fish that require a careful approach and a delicate presentation, especially if they are lying shallow. The river has also changed character in the farmland section, having suffered from a huge flood in 1997. Some of the long riffles have disappeared and there is now more broken water. One previous riffle will always stay in my memory — a 500 metre-long run that you could wade up quite easily, casting to rises left and right. One hot February afternoon I spotted over twenty fish up this stretch, about half of them on the rise. They were taking freely, and it took me three hours to cover the distance, hooking ten fish on the way. Such magic days are to be treasured — they are becoming rather scarce.

Relating this particular experience to my Wanganui mate Bill, convinced him it was time he tried out his skills on the wily South Island brown. We booked into a comfortable new motel just up the road from Springs Junction, and I thought the Blue Grey would prove an appropriate place to start Bill's mainland fishing education. The water around Springs Junction has some of the highest concentrations of brown trout in New Zealand, so we knew we were in the right place. The motel owner confirmed this by telling us about a visitor from Idaho who had landed a 10-pounder not far down the river from Lake Christabel.

Bill and I started in the area just before the 'Private Property' sign on Palmer Road. I knew this stretch was popular with the local guides, which is usually a good indicator, as those guys have to produce fish for their paying customers. Despite a dram or three the night before, we managed an early start and were on the water by 8 o'clock. There were no other vehicles along the road and we were pleased to have the river all to ourselves.

I took Bill through a copse of big beech trees to the first pool above the gorge that extends all the way down to the Robinson River. We crept to the edge of the trees and stared intently into the greeny-blue water. Towards the middle of the pool, a metre in front of a boulder, I spied a grey smudge. It was a good-sized brown feeding at about a metre deep. It always pays to look for feeding trout in front of rocks as well as behind them. Nearly as many lie there as are to be found sheltering from the flow in the more obvious spot.

Bill said it was my fish, so I left the trees and sidled down to the edge of the tail. In a half crouch, I cautiously crept up the pool until I could see the 'smudge'. It was feeding away happily. Having marked its position, I backed away a couple of metres. Kneeling down, I once again praised the designer of my polar-fleece fishing pants for including knee patches. This is the usual 'assumed position' for casting to the wily mainland browns.

My rig consisted of a 2.5 m tapered fluorocarbon leader and a further 1.5 m of tippet. I let out several metres of line into the current with a lightly weighted size 12 beadhead Pheasant Tail. It took a while for the line to straighten in the current, then I was able to flick the 5 weight line forward. I had learned on my previous visit that false-casting over the head of spooky browns was guaranteed to scare them. The calm of the morning allowed an accurate cast for a change, and the fly plopped in gently about 2 m above the trout. It would need that distance to sink to the fish's depth.

I could no longer see my quarry from my low position, so I was relying on the small yarn indicator at the tippet junction, 1.5 m up from the fly. It moved sharply, and I tightened on a surprised trout. It shot up strongly to the head of the pool, obviously heading for his usual bolt-hole under the rocks there. Some serious sidestrain managed to turn it before it got there, and we settled down to fight it out in the middle of the pool. Expect a good battle from a Blue Grey brown as they are tough fish; they need to be to survive in this flood-prone river. Fortunately for me, the middle of

'Beech tree' pool on the Blue Grey.

the pool held no more escape opportunities, and a few runs later a beautifully spotted 2.5 kg brown was wallowing in the shallows, ready for release. A promising start to the day.

Bill and I were walking up the bank to the next reach just as a ute came down the road. I gave a friendly wave but it wasn't reciprocated. Perhaps the guide at the wheel didn't feel so friendly at missing out on his chosen starting spot. He made a U-turn and trundled off up the road with his two clients. I knew this meant we would not have a long stretch of water available to us, so we would have to fish slowly and thoroughly, examining every likely lie with care. Too often I have raced through unlikely looking water and spooked fish in unexpected places.

Bill's first fish came at the next pool — a deep, wide one. We concealed ourselves in the beech trees while we looked down into the azure depths. The water's clarity did the fish no favours. It was easy to spot a grey smudge about 10 m out, feeding actively at the bottom, 3 m down. Something heavy would be needed to catch this denizen of the deep.

I pulled open the fly box and looked for a bit of weight. A size 8 Stonefly caught my eye. Handing it to Bill, I advised him to put on a size 14 Pheasant Tail as a tail fly in case stoneflies were out of favour. He moved out to the edge of the trees, where he could get casting room but still be hidden from the trout. It took him a few casts to get the nymphs into the particular tongue of water bringing food to the bottom dweller, but the first drift in the right place saw the fish move towards the nymph. The indicator dipped satisfyingly, and Bill struck hard. Another surprised brown shot upstream. Bill turned the first headlong charge and they settled down to a decent joust in the middle of the pool. Before too long, Bill had the 2 kg fish on the bank for a quick photo, then a flick of the forceps set it free.

The most notable fish of the day was taken 'blind' from some good-looking water on the far side of the river. The crossing was a bit hairy even with my Leki wading stick in full use. However, with some raucous encouragement from Bill, I managed to cross the tail of the pool without giving him the pleasure of seeing me take an early bath.

Halfway up the pool, a stream emerged from the forest and tumbled into the river. I stood in the trees on the bank for a few minutes but could spot nothing. After all that effort to cross the river, though, I just had to put a few drifts through the pool. It was a difficult one to fish, as the stream had carved deep when it had been in flood and scattered large rocks along the bottom. As a result, there was a lot of turbulence, which quickly pulled the fly down and dragged the small indicator under.

I decided to use a heavier fly to ensure I got to the bottom of the pool. Rummaging through my fly box, I noticed another weighted Stonefly and figured that if it had worked for Bill, it could work for me. I reattached the size 14 Pheasant Tail nymph to the bend of the sinker fly. Now I needed to lengthen the leader to ensure I got the fly down to the bottom of the pool. The quickest way to do this was to remove the small yarn indicator and snap on a foam one at the leader junction. This meant the leader was effectively 1.5 m longer, and the bigger indicator would mean I could see any unnatural changes to the drift more easily through the turbulent water.

On the second pass the indicator seemed to hesitate, and I struck hard, knowing I needed to straighten the long leader. For a split second I thought I had snagged one of the rocks on the bottom, then a very angry large brown erupted from the pool and splashed down heavily. It raced 50 m up to the head of the pool and dived into the rock face, just as its smaller mate downstream had tried to do. They must teach this escape technique in trout school. This time it worked, and nothing I could do would persuade the fish to exit its bolt-hole. The old trick of giving it slack line wasn't possible as the current pulling on the line was too strong and negated that ploy. I suppose I could have waited it out but I suspected that could have taken all day and I would rather be fishing than sitting on a bank. Regretfully, I pulled out the fly and was left to wonder at the size of that brown: our encounter had certainly proved there were a few big ones left in the river.

I was brought out of my reverie by shouts of derision from across the water, from where Bill had observed the action. I stretched my arms a metre apart to let him know the size of the fish was the reason for its loss, not a lack of skill on my part. But this produced only more expressions of disbelief. One day I must find more sympathetic fishing partners.

Not being keen on another precarious crossing, I proceeded along the bank to the next pool. It wasn't possible to walk at river level, the bank being 3 m high. Fortunately, bushbashing in beech forest is a lot more pleasant than in the Kaweka equivalent. The lack of undergrowth makes for easier progress and less chance of a rod-breaking stumble. The river was wider and shallower for a long way up, so it was time to remove the sinker nymph and the foam indicator.

My success rate had improved a lot when I had learned to adapt my rig to the depth and speed of water I was fishing. As these change, it is advisable to alter your terminal tackle. You may need to change the leader length to suit the depth and the weight of your fly to suit the current. The quickest way of changing your leader length is simply to move the indicator. The shallower the fish is lying, the nearer your indicator should be to the fly. Reading a recent article by Tony Orman, I was pleasantly surprised to find he had reached the same conclusion — no doubt many years before. When you receive affirmation of a personal theory from the guru of nymphing in New Zealand, you know you are on the right track.

The easiest way of adapting to the speed of the current is to change the weight of your fly. For many years, I have preferred to do this by using a sinker fly with a small, more-likely-to-be-taken fly attached to the bend of the larger hook. If a fish is lying deep, it is unlikely to be put off by the larger fly, and it is surprising just how often a fish will in fact take the larger fly by preference. Rainbows are generally more likely to do this, but often a big brown will also be tempted by a large Stonefly nymph, sometimes when all else has failed. As soon as you come to a shallower stretch, it is a simple matter to remove the double flies and tie on a single small fly. That was the call for prospecting the bubbly riffle ahead, so on went a size 14 beadhead Hare'n'Copper. However, the long pool yielded only one 2 kg hen, which was a bit disappointing considering I was on the less popular side of the river. Maybe all the locals are reckless waders and work on the same theory. On later visits it has been noticeable that the larger fish do lie on the far side of the river, protected by the cover of the beech trees. Some big fish, in excess of 4 kg, have been spotted at the edge of the large pools near the top of the gorge. They were all in the shade of the trees and were obviously more comfortable there rather than on the more open road side.

On that day with Bill, the fish were scarce but the serenity and beauty of the forest more than made up for that. I took my time working up the riffle while bellbirds and tui serenaded me. At several places where there was access to the river, the only tracks I saw were those of a deer that had come down for a drink at dusk or dawn. But pausing often to admire the surroundings was doing little for my fishing concentration, so I decided to sit down for a rest and to give the scenery the appreciation it deserved.

My peace was soon interrupted by abuse from across the river as Bill drew level. He wanted to exchange notes, so I found a safe crossing place and rejoined him. He had picked up a couple of fish in the 1.5–2 kg range so was keen to bend my ear for an hour on how his great expertise had triumphed over the difficult Blue Grey trout. As usual, I was happy to listen because good fishing companions are hard to come by. It is not

The Blue Grey River.

much fun to fish with someone who fishes too fast or too slow, or disturbs the water, or is much better than you are, or much worse, or talks too much or not enough. So you tend to treasure a good fishing mate who has proven his compatibility over many excursions.

Continuing upriver, it wasn't long before we reached the spot where footprints showed where the guided party had started in. We didn't see any more trout from that point on. It is quite likely we relaxed a little and saw nothing because that was what we were expecting. It is always hard to concentrate on fishing in such an idyllic setting. You may even see a couple of kaka fly overhead — one of the last breeding pairs in the area. Certainly the silent beech forest that carpets the far bank looks as though it has remained untouched for centuries.

In places like this any fish are a bonus, so don't despair if you spook the only trout you have seen all day. Just round the corner there could be a deep blue pool with something hovering a metre below the surface — a grey smudge!

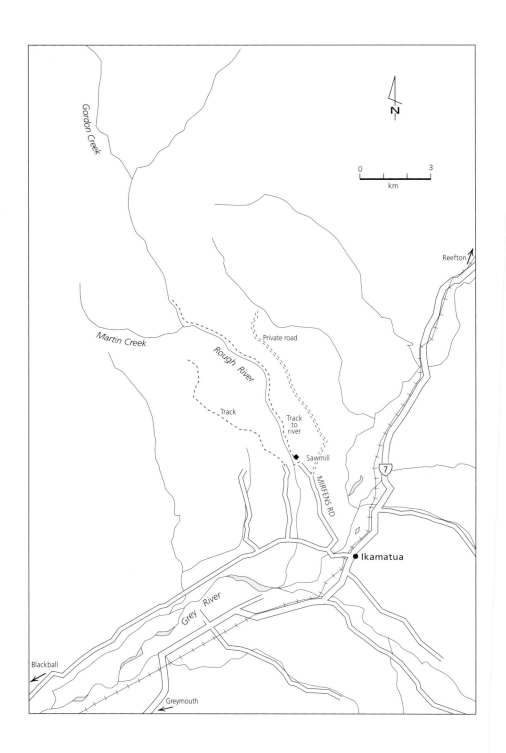

Gordon Creek

Martin Creek

Rough River

Private road

Track

Track
to
river

Sawmill

MIRFENS RD

7

Reefton

Ikamatua

Grey River

Blackball

Greymouth

0 — 3
km

N

Rough River
Double-fly rigs and their use

DESCRIPTION AND DIRECTIONS

The Rough River starts its life on the eastern side of the Paparoa Range on the West Coast, north of Greymouth. It then flows for about 30 km on a southeasterly course to join the mighty Grey River near Ikamatua. To a few fly-fishers, mainly locals and fishing guides, it is known for the size of its trout. The reason they grow so big is the river's remoteness and inaccessibility. There is only one road to the lower reaches, and to fish the middle or upper reaches involves a long walk or the hire of a helicopter. The Paparoa Range has no road or even track access — true wilderness country.

The east of the range forms the catchment feeding the various Grey River tributaries, which can be accessed by farm roads only to their lower reaches. One of these is Mirfens Road, which ends at an entrance to a sawmill, where it is necessary to park your car and walk 200 m down to the river. The Rough River is quite wide at this point, and it is usually easiest to sidle along the bank beside the sawmill. Once past the mill, the river is easier to cross, and many crossings are needed to progress up the wide valley. Be warned: the going is very hard. The stones underfoot are mainly flattish spheres and very unstable.

After a kilometre or so, the river swings to the left and is very swift. It doesn't look like good holding water, and it pays to push on beyond where 'part-day' anglers tend to reach. You will come to a large island, where the river has cut a new course in recent years. Above this, the river flows through an open valley. The water here is more stable, although braided in typical South Island fashion, so the pools are far apart. This means a lot of walking, and it is vital to inspect each piece of water thoroughly or you may overlook the only fish for several hundred metres.

About 5 km above the island are some cliffs on the right. Here the water is a little more stable still, being confined to the side along the cliffs. Above this stretch is the province of camping anglers and helicopters, the latter providing the easiest means past the two steep gorges that restrict foot progress to all but the fittest of anglers.

The lower stretches of the river are accessed by heading downstream from the sawmill or by driving back down to Atarau Road and along to the bridge over the Rough. There is a good half-day's fishing from the bridge up to the sawmill. The water is even more braided than higher up, and there is a lot of walking between fishable spots. Good trout are to be found but, being relatively accessible, they attract more angling pressure. Accordingly, the best fishing is early or late in the day, when the browns are a little more venturesome. The average weight is around 1.5 kg, with the possibility of the occasional bigger catch.

Below the bridge, there's about 2 km of braided water before you reach the Grey River. However, in these lower reaches, in the middle of the day, it is possible to clearly see the bottom of most pools, and the trout tend to seek cover until the light is less strong. As access is easy from the road, it is advisable to fish in the evening, when the trout are more likely to be out in the open and there is a good chance of picking up a trophy fish.

TALES AND TECHNIQUES

Many rivers are easier to fish than the Rough. Because of the lack of access, there is a lot of walking to be done to find a sizeable fish. Most of this is over round, flattened rocks dumped precariously on top of one another by the last flood. They are just lying in wait for the footfall of the next unwary angler. If you put in the hard work, though, and take care of your ankles, you might get a chance at a really good fish.

The best place to start is above the island, about two hours' walk up from the end of Mirfens Road, as there are some good pools in the next kilometre or so. The first time I fished the Rough, I reached this point at around 9 o'clock, having made an unusually early start. The sun was still hunkered down below the tree line, and the pool before me was in shadow. As there was no chance of spotting fish in that light, I had to fish 'blind'. I put on the trusty two-fly rig, with about 30 cm between the flies. This rig has seen a lot of use since my beginner days on the Tongariro. For blind-nymphing smaller rivers, it works well with a lightly weighted size 12 beadhead Hare'n'Copper and an unweighted size 14 or 16 tail fly tied to the bend of the hook of the weighted fly. Good trout do not often take the bigger fly, but I suspect the intrusion of the beadhead attracts their atten-tion. When they take a look at it, they see the smaller fly trundling along behind and think it looks more like the real thing.

Normally, 20 cm between flies is about right, depending on the wind. If there is no wind, you can lengthen the distance so the tail fly moves more naturally. However, when the wind gets up, there is a good chance of tangling the two flies during casting, and you will find a 20 cm gap minimises frustration.

On that day, I decided the tail fly should be a size 14 Pheasant Tail, as I had seen plenty of mayfly nymphs under rocks on my way up the river. I started in at the tail of a long, wide pool with a fishy-looking riffle running down the middle. A couple of casts and I had a problem. I had on a brand-new olive-green fly line that my fishing-tackle guru, John Giacon, had assured me could not be seen on the water. He was right. But this also meant that, in the poor light, I would not be able to see the line move when a take occurred. It was necessary to reel in and attach an indicator.

In such delicate waters, I prefer the style favoured by South Island guides, especially those in the heavily fished waters of the Nelson area. They use a snippet of synthetic yarn only about 1 cm long. A good rule of thumb is to make the indicator roughly the same size as the fly you are using. Tie it in at the junction of the trace nylon to tapered leader, 1–2 m from the fly. If you want the indicator at a different place from the looped junction, it is best to tie a clove hitch in the leader and slip the piece of yarn into the middle of the knot. Then pull tight, and the yarn will be firmly held until you want to move or remove it. To do so, simply push against the clove hitch from each end and the knot easily comes undone.

Indicator tied in with clove hitch.

This positioning of the indicator gives you a closer contact with the fly, and you can see takes much more quickly. It doesn't seem to spook the trout, as rises to the indicator are common. That innovative fly-tier Hughie McDowell invented a bright red/orange dry fly because he was having so many rises to his yarn indicator!

There is no doubt you can miss a lot of takes with the indicator positioned 3 or 4 m from the fly. This is easily proven if you sit high on a bank and watch someone fishing with a long leader up a deep, clear run. From your elevated position, you will see a fish take and wonder why the angler hasn't struck. Often the fish will spit out the nymph before the angler detects what is happening. This is because of the time it takes a leader to straighten, especially in turbulent water, resulting in a considerable delay before the indicator moves. The nearer you have your indicator to your fly, the quicker you will see a take.

On went the tiny indicator, and I resumed fishing up the centre riffle. The second cast up the run yielded a sudden dip of the indicator. Lifting the rod, I fastened into a good fish. It surged across the river, not at any great speed but with the power of a big fish. It seemed confident that this minor irritation would soon be dealt with and it could resume breakfasting before too long.

The far bank was more than 30 m away, and I was concerned I had a lot of line in the water, which meant the flexibility of the rod wasn't available to handle any sudden moves on the fish's part. I could feel the strain of the current on the long line submerged in the water. There was no point in applying sidestrain as I had too much line out to get enough leverage, so I climbed up to the top of the 3 m high shingle bank behind me. This enabled me to retrieve a lot of line and get in reasonably direct contact with the fish. Now I applied some careful sidestrain, and the fish responded by turning into the faster water in the centre of the run. That suited me fine, as I could see no snags or rocks that it might use to gain an advantage. Twenty minutes and a few adventures later I had my largest-ever trout in the shallows below. I estimated the weight at over 6 kg. My best up to then had been one of 5.5 kg from the Ruakituri, and this brown hen looked a lot bigger.

To get a photo I was going to have to lift my catch up to the top of the high stony bank. I hesitated, because just the night before I had been reading a Canadian study on mortality rates among fish that had been caught and released. It had found the mortality rate doubled if fish were out of the water for more than 30 seconds, which means many of those shots you see of anglers holding up their catch for a photo session possibly resulted in a dead fish. As this had to be one of the biggest fish in the river, I decided not to take the risk. I carefully picked my way down the bank, leaned down and freed the fly with my forceps. The big hen didn't need coaxing to swim away, so the theory seemed sound.

I then sat down for a while to savour the moment and replay the whole event in my mind. It was still only 9.30 am, and the goal for the day had already been well and truly achieved. The memory of the dorsal fin of that huge fish cutting through the shallow water will be in my mind's creel forever. There can't be too many places in the world where an average angler can catch a fish that size without a guide or a helicopter, just two strong legs to get about on. Reading how Americans get excited about hooking a 'trophy' 18-incher (perhaps 3 lbs/1.4 kg) makes you appreciate what we have in this country. Whether we are appreciative enough and do all we should to protect what we have is a matter that demands constant debate.

The attraction of this particular riffle to large fish was further demonstrated one early November morning two years later when an 11 lb (5 kg) brown also took a size 14 Pheasant Tail. That fish was hooked at 7.45 am, proving that an early start is essential on this river if you want to catch a big fish.

As you progress up the Rough's braided middle reaches, where pools are few and far between, it is essential to inspect every piece of water that might hold a fish, as it is often surprising where fish lie. This is particularly so early in the morning or in the evening, when the low light will entice trout into the shallows to graze on nymphs. As soon as the light is stronger, they move back to where there is more cover. However, there is no cover for the angler, so it is necessary to stay well back from the pools, kneeling down with the bank behind so you are not silhouetted against the sky. Although sometimes the water can have a touch of that typical West Coast peaty colour, trout are easy to spot in the small, clear pools. The browns may be well camouflaged against the browny-olive rocks, though, so it is advisable to take your time and really examine every pool.

Several kilometres further up are some cliffs on the true right bank. Here there are some better-defined pools, as the water is confined along one side by the cliffs rather than winding aimlessly across the wide flood plain, as it does below here. It isn't possible for the day-fisher to spend long here, though, as this is about as far as you can fish without overnighting. It is a long, arduous walk back to the car park. I never cease to be amazed by the distance one can cover when absorbed by fishing, and just how far this proves to be for tired legs on the way home. Those unstable stones are even more dangerous when you're weary: I recall ending up on my backside a couple of times that day. On such occasions the 'fanny pack' style of fishing vest has an added advantage.

Make sure you are back at your car before 5.00 pm if you have parked down by the river. The sawmill closes around then and the gate is locked with a padlocked chain. If, like I did, you ignore the instructions in the guidebook to park in the paddock before the gate, you might be panicking a bit on your return. Fortunately for me, this time there was no padlock on the chain and a long, cold night was avoided. A local farmer informed me the padlock had been broken on so many occasions that the mill had given up using one. I'm not sure if the problem was workers breaking out or anglers breaking in to get at the superb water.

If the upper valley sounds a bit strenuous, the lower stretches still offer some quality fishing. From the sawmill down to the road bridge, there are some nice pools and many interesting riffles. Thanks to the regular West Coast downpours, the river enjoys good flow levels even through summer.

The 14-pounder riffle.

In fact, as with most West Coast rivers, finding it not in flood is a real bonus if you have travelled far to get there. It pays to venture to the Coast only during settled weather, as there is nothing worse than being cooped up in a motel waiting for the rain to ease and the rivers to clear.

Downstream from the road bridge gives a satisfying day's fishing. You can make your way down the Rough until you meet the Grey. Spend an hour or two pottering around there, then fish back up the Rough in the early evening looking for some dry-fly action. This is a good time to put on a combo dry fly/nymph rig and prospect the faster riffles. Fish are more likely to be feeding there in the evening, and an Irresistible or Humpy dancing down may indeed prove more than a trout can ignore.

The Irresistible is always a good choice for the dry on a combo rig. It is a simple pattern that rides high and will support a light nymph as a tail fly. Those deer-hair flies work well in rough water, having good floating characteristics.

Irresistible

Hook: size 12
Tail: brown bucktail
Body: natural deer hair spun on the hook, then clipped to a barrel shape
Wing: two grizzle tips pointing upwards
Hackle: one grizzle, one badger-cock feather

One late summer evening, a mate and I picked up six good trout fishing up from the Grey River using a dry fly/nymph combo rig. Although the fish were not obviously rising, several took the dry fly in preference to the nymph. As the light fades, it is useful to have a dry fly that can be seen more easily. A tuft of white calftail incorporated into standard rough-water flies helps considerably to make the indicator dry fly visible. The chances of picking up a fish or two are certainly better in the subdued evening light.

Along most of the Rough River, if you pick up a couple of trout, you will have had a worthwhile day. And there will probably have been a lot of water in between. This is not the sort of river where you chance upon a pool full of trout; it is a river that rewards hours of hard walking and meticulous study of every stretch that might just hold a fish. As there are not too many waters that can yield fish of comparable quality, it is likely to be worth the effort.

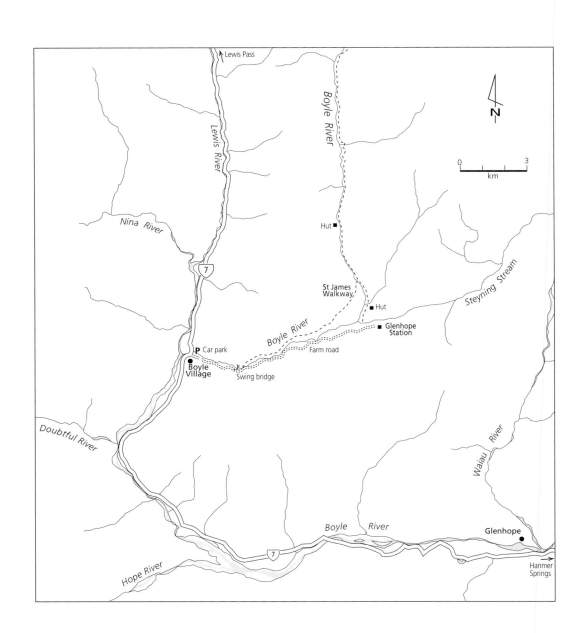

Boyle River
Fishing for sea-run trout

DESCRIPTION AND DIRECTIONS

The Boyle River is probably better known to trampers than to trout-fishers. This is because the popular St James Walkway follows the river for much of its course. Starting at a car park near the highway bridge over the river, the track wends its way through beautiful beech forest, crossing the river a kilometre or so upstream. It then winds through the bush alongside the river for another 3 km to meet the main tributary, the Steyning Stream. Above here, the upper river is much smaller and continues up the valley between the Opera and Libretto ranges. Most of the Boyle and its tributary lie within the boundaries of Glenhope Station, and, historically, foot access has been allowed.

The Boyle is joined by the Lewis River, near the main Lewis Pass highway (SH 7). It continues down the valley, the Nina, Doubtful and Hope rivers adding to its flow, before it meets the Waiau River near Glenhope. The Waiau is the source of the silvery sea-run brown trout frequently found in the Boyle when conditions are right.

The lower part of the Boyle is fishable from the Hope confluence up, with access from the main road. This crosses the river just up from the Lewis confluence. There is a car park on the right before the bridge, and the river can be fished from here up. The first section consists of a rugged gorge with small, deep pools that are a precise miniature of those to be found on much bigger rivers. The gorge is easily accessed as the banks are gentle and there is a path through the beech trees, just above the river. Usually the pools are full of fish, albeit mostly small ones. It is ideal water for the novice fly-fisher, the small fish taking voraciously and giving a good account of themselves. The character of the water remains much the same up to where a swing bridge crosses the river 2 km from the car park.

The next section consists of more bouldery, boisterous pocket water that requires a different approach from the relatively heavier water downstream. The fish here are a bit bigger; most are of a legal size, with an average weight of around 1 kg. Fishing is best before the sun creeps over the beech-clad hills, as the trout feed freely until the sun exposes their shallow lies.

A kilometre or so further up, damage from a colossal flood a few years ago is obvious. A shingle fan, created when the incoming stream was in flood, spreads out to a width of 100 m, and has filled in several of the productive pools that used to be found here. The result is a faster stretch of water with no holes to shelter trout. It is best to bypass the area and walk on to where the track veers to the left. Here there are a couple of excellent runs, and these are nearly always frequented by one or two reasonable trout, sometimes even a big sea-run brown.

Above these pools, the river divides in two with the Steyning Stream going up the wide valley on the right. The river above the junction is much smaller and requires a change of tactics, as the fish are now very spottable. There being no deep pools, they lie out in the open in the shallow riffles and runs, so a stealthy approach is essential. Despite this, there are often 1–2 kg trout along this stretch, but they tend to be well apart, meaning long walks in between. It is possible to fish a long way up the valley, but the water becomes very low in summer and it is probably not worth the effort except early or late in the season.

TALES AND TECHNIQUES

The Boyle can be a frustrating river, and the fishing varies from season to season. When I first fished it, it had much deeper holes in the middle reaches, which meant there was cover for the large sea-run browns from the Waiau. A fishing mate, Peter Witteman, had discovered this when he had caught a 4.5 kg brown in the gorge not far up from the track car park. One night, when I was dining at his home in Kaiapoi, he pulled the fish out of the freezer, where it resided, waiting for mounting. Even in its frozen state it looked magnificent: a beautiful deep fish, with pale-brown spots along its silvery flanks. It was the first sea-run brown I had ever seen, and I was impressed, so little discussion was needed when Peter offered to take me to the river the following weekend.

We decided to stay at the historic Hurunui Hotel, as this is about an hour up the road from Christchurch and would cut down the travelling time. The Saturday saw us up early and off on the one-hour journey to the Boyle River. We reached the car park around 8 o'clock and tackled up. Pete was very serious about his trout-fishing and had picked up a few tips at his local fly-fishing

The lower
Boyle.

club meetings. One of these was that a shiny rod finish could flash when fishing in sunlight. To eliminate this possibility, he had coated his new rod with a matt, camouflage-colour paint. At the time I thought it was a shame to ruin such a lovely rod but have changed my opinion over the years.

We proceeded up the gorge, walking through the beech forest that borders the river on both sides in the lower stretches. Pete showed me the pool, not far below the swing bridge, where he caught his big fish. Despite some tempting drifts through the pool, nothing came to his fly this time. We fished all the way up the gorge, and where it opened out there were some lovely pools, broken up by big boulders. It looked like good fish-holding water. Pete invited me to have a go while he tried the riffles and pools above.

The second of the two pools saw a fish take as the nymph drifted into the quiet water behind a boulder. After a short but hard fight, I eased the trout into the shallows. At first I thought it was a rainbow, as its sides flashed silver in the sun. But on closer examination, I could clearly see the pale spots of a brown. I paused for a moment to admire the gleaming flank of the 1.5 kg hen before releasing it back into the water. After fishing the area thoroughly, with no more success, I walked along the track until I caught up with Pete. We swapped success stories, then I said I would walk on a kilometre or two to give him some fishing room.

Continuing along the walkway for about twenty minutes, I came to the point where the valley opened up. The walkway veered off to the left, staying in the cover of the beech forest, while the river carried straight on.

I crossed over at the tail of a pool and walked along the bank above a slow-ish, deep run below the mouth of a major tributary. Fortunately, I was taking my time and able to come to a sudden halt as I saw a flash in the rocky depths. I froze, slowly knelt down and peered into the water. Two large fish were feeding 2 m deep in the run.

Studying the situation, I felt that casting from the bank would be likely to spook the fish. Any motion as you are silhouetted against the horizon is bound to be noticed by fish, even if they are lying quite deep. I decided to retreat downstream to the tail of the pool and crossed back over. Moving up the shingle bank, I soon reached the point a few metres below the bush I had chosen as a marker. I put on a size 12 weighted Flashback nymph linked to a size 14 unweighted Pheasant Tail.

I measured the distance and threw up a cast. It landed in the right area but more on my side of the river than I wanted. The next cast was further across, and I threw a quick downstream mend for drag, as the current was stronger near the far bank. As the line drifted past the marker bush, the indicator stopped suddenly, and a millisecond later a large fish tore off downstream.

I played it carefully as I could see it was big — possibly a 'double'. There wasn't much help for the fish as the banks were free of obstructions, with just shingle on my side, and fifteen minutes later we were battling it out at the tail of the pool. The gleaming silver fish showed great interest in heading off downstream for the Waiau River, but heaps of sidestrain saw it stranded on a tongue of rocks where the river split in two. It was a beautiful silver-sided brown hen that lay flapping on the shingle. I measured her quickly against the rod and freed the Pheasant Tail from her jaw. She finned off quickly upstream, sending a bow wave through the shallow water. I sat down and measured the mark on the rod: 31 inches (85 cm). Surely a 10-pounder! My first in the South Island.

Still shaking a bit, I took a while to gather my thoughts before setting off back up the pool. As the fish had run downstream, there was a chance it hadn't disturbed the other occupant of the pool. I retied the same flies and moved up to my bush marker.

The first couple of casts produced nothing and I decided the second fish must have been spooked. However, the next drift through saw the indicator stop again. Another large silver bullet shot downstream and fifteen minutes later was beached in the same place. It was the same size, too: 31 inches. It was hard to believe this small river could produce two such large fish from the same pool. Beginner's luck, obviously. At least, that was what

Pete called it when I rejoined him a couple of pools further down. He hadn't had quite the same good fortune but was pleased I had done so well on his favourite stream. We decided to call it quits for the day and head back to the pub for a celebratory Speights.

Having met with some success, we felt compelled to return the next day for another crack at the super silvers. There were no more double-figure fish but I did pick up another five trout, making a return for the weekend of ten fish from the small river. Weights ranged from 1.5 kg to 4.5 kg plus for the two big ones. All were silver sea-run browns, so we must have struck a run.

Sea-runs are a strange fish to predict. Originally, fish scientists thought they were a separate strain of trout, but the current theory is that they were one of the many different brown-trout species introduced over 100 years ago and have since interbred with river fish because they share the same spawning grounds. Scientists now believe some of the hatched fish drop back down to the sea while others stay upriver. No one can come up with a theory as to why this variance in behaviour should occur. There is undoubtedly more food in the sea, and sea-run trout grow faster and larger than their river-confined cousins, reaching 4.5 kg at only three years of age while river browns can take twice as long to attain the same weight.

When the sea-dwelling browns reach maturity at three or four years old, they move up the rivers to the headwaters, where they spawn during late autumn and early winter. From this meagre information, it would seem the best time to catch a large sea-run is late summer or early autumn, during the move upriver. However, the trout we caught in the Boyle were taken in November — the same time of year as the well-known annual run of large sea trout up the Pomohaka River in Otago. Similar runs occur in other Canterbury rivers, even during the low flows of summer. So it would appear sea-run browns move upriver at much the same time as their larger cousins, Quinnat salmon.

The next visit to the Boyle proved the unreliability of sea-runs. I had brought a group of Aucklanders after regaling them with stories of the huge fish, but as usual, reality failed to meet the expectations raised by my (mostly unembroidered) tales. I shouldn't have promised so much. Despite fishing the river from the start of the gorge right up to the open valley, we didn't see a single fish. Since my earlier visit, there had been a massive flood. Few deep stretches remained, meaning there was little cover for fish. We could see clearly into the deepest of the pools in the upper section that I fished, and the guys who tried the deeper pools in the

A silver-sided
sea-run brown.

gorge connected with zilch. They were experienced nymphers who could competently fish deep pools, so it seemed the browns had deserted the Boyle and retreated to the Waiau.

Since then, the river has been getting back to its old self. The pools in the gorge are again deep enough to shelter good-sized fish. It is best to be on the river early and to fish up through the gorge before the sun gets high enough to hit the water. The best technique is to blind-nymph the pools by casting into the rapids at the head so the nymphs sink quickly into the eye of the pool. The fish will either be holding in the eye or just to the side in the quieter water at the seam. Either way, they will take freely if a neutral-coloured line is drifted through the centre. This is not difficult fishing, and suits beginners or kids. Many fish are small, and a good proportion illegal, but that never worries those who haven't caught many trout before. Any sort of beadhead sinker, with a small brown tail fly, will be voraciously gulped by these enthusiastic youngsters.

But always be prepared for something larger. My last visit to the river saw a big fish take my fly in the large pool the locals call 'the Pond'. It was a solid take but the connection was short-lived. However, it was enough for me to be thinking that the sea-runs could be up the river. It was with a heightened sense of anticipation that I approached the next pool.

This was a short but deep pool that curved around a large boulder halfway down. It had a very turbulent top section with the result that the first few drifts through did not seem to be getting deep enough. I knew that sea–runs preferred the security afforded by the very bottom of a pool, so it would require a change of tackle to solve the problem. Off came the yarn indicator and on went a foam one two metres further up the leader. On also went a heavy size 10 Caddis with a size 14 beadhead trailing along. Second cast into the depths of the pool was met by a solid take. A strong fish surged up the current to the head of the pool and a dogged fight then ensued. At times I seemed to be winning and was able to at least get the fish close enough to see that it was a double figure silver sea-run brown. Just when I was mentally picturing what a fine photo the fish would make, it made a violent final surge up the pool. And was gone. I reeled in. The tail fly was missing and the 2.5 kg leader cleanly snapped.

'Oh well', I said (or words to that effect). It was interesting that the theory of a November/December timing for the entry of the sea-run browns was confirmed — it was the first of December.

Above the gorge it is necessary to change techniques. Here the water consists mainly of rocky riffles. So long as the sun is not on the water, the browns lie quite shallow and are hard to see in the turbulent riffles, even though most are only a metre deep. It's time to take off the two-fly rig and put on a single, lightly weighted size 12–14 (beadhead) Hare'n'Copper. In fact, the bead is probably all the weight you need. Tungsten beads are heavy enough to avoid having any lead in the tie, which is better for the environment too. Cast the beadhead up to the top of a short riffle and let it wend its way around the many rock obstructions. You don't even need to concentrate too hard; the take will be fierce and the trout will virtually hook itself. In this stretch, the trout average only a kilo or so, but they fight well and any young angler will enjoy chasing a silver bullet downstream — 'Just like Dad does, Mum!'

By the time you reach the valley, the sun will be on the water and it will be time to change techniques again. Here the beginner will struggle, while the experienced 'stalker' will do better. Maybe this is the time for Junior to watch and learn from the old man. The fish lie in the deeper riffles and runs but can be spotted easily. Unfortunately, so can the angler. The conditions call for a slow, careful approach to any potentially fish-holding water. Casting has to be kept to a minimum, and one of Pete's non-flash rods would come in handy. A long, thin leader and a single, lightly weighted fly are also essential. The riffly water will disguise some error in allowing for drag, but a light landing of the line is necessary.

It is best to cast into the faster water in the middle of a riffle as the fish hold in the deeper water where the current isn't as strong. Mending is hardly required; just retrieve the line as it comes towards you so there is no loose line between you and the fly. A small yarn indicator, positioned a metre up from the fly, will prove most efficient in the shallow, bubbly flow.

So long as you stay in touch with your fly, a quick lift of the rod will set the hook. Just remember this is not a big river where a strong strike is essential. Such a strike here can produce the embarrassing sight of a 10 cm fingerling catapulting far into the trees behind you, which may result in a significant lowering of your reputation with any bankside audience. A handsome silver sea-run brown, on the other hand, will see your reputation considerably enhanced. You can then relax for the evening while your offspring tell all and sundry about 'Dad's big silver fish!'

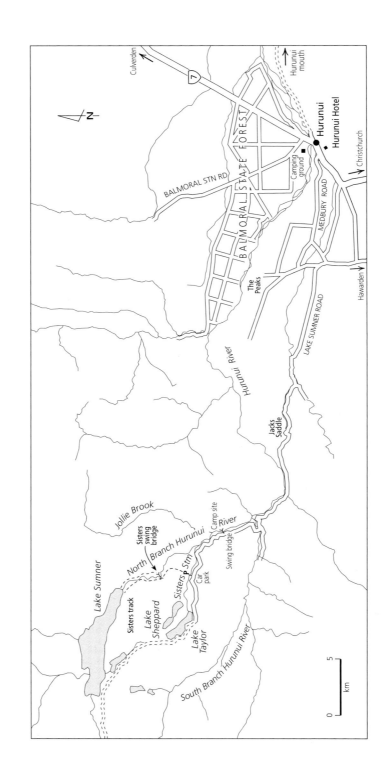

Hurunui River
Prospecting and shotgunning techniques

DESCRIPTION AND DIRECTIONS

The big, brawling Hurunui River is as well known to Canterbury salmon-fishers as it is to trout-anglers. It has one of the earlier runs of the eastern salmon rivers, but most of the activity is around the mouth, south of Cheviot. The lower section of the river, from Balmoral Forest down, is a typical braided Canterbury river with a constantly changing course. This does not appeal much to brown trout, as they prefer a more stable environment. There is some good fishing below the main highway bridge, but the trout are mainly found in the backwaters, especially under the willows. They are very wary in the still water, so great stealth is required. Access is easy down Hurunui Bluff Road just before the SH 7 bridge when heading north.

Around Balmoral, the river can be accessed from Tekoa Road to the north and The Peaks Station to the south. It is still very braided in this area and much walking is required to find fish, but there is the occasional sizeable one where the river is more stable.

Above here, there is no access for many kilometres as the river enters a long gorge. The only way to the upper reaches is via the road to Lake Sumner. This is a long, winding, gravel road on which care must be taken, as accidents are common. It rejoins the river at the top of the gorge. Access is possible by scrambling down the steep banks, but the flow is heavy and only the edges are fly-fisher territory.

A few hundred metres further up is another short gorge, above which there is good nymphing water all the way up to the confluence of the South Branch. This tributary is worth fishing early and late in the season, although access is limited by an impassable gorge not far upstream. The South Branch colours the Hurunui after rain, but being lake-fed the upper river remains clear above the confluence, and a stable flow is assured most of the time.

Above the confluence is where most fly-fishing is done. The countryside here has a raw and rugged feel as the river flows through matagouri- and tussock-clad hills. There are designated 'anglers' access' points along the road and plenty of riffles and runs to prospect. Trout average 1.5 kg, with many bigger ones caught. The Jollie Brook junction area is very popular, particularly at holiday time, when campers adorn the banks. The river here is difficult to wade but there is a swing bridge a little further down.

Above here, the road leaves the river and heads over the hill to Lake Sheppard. At the bottom of the hill there is a gate, and on the right is a foot track to the Sisters Stream area. This is perhaps the most productive stretch of the whole river, and it is possible to fish all the way up to the lake. There are also a couple of 4WD tracks that can be negotiated to reach the area below the outlet. The Upper Hurunui River flows into Lake Sumner but access is restricted to tramping anglers.

The main problem when fishing the Hurunui is the dreaded Canterbury nor'wester. Even if there isn't much wind elsewhere, by mid-afternoon there can be a gale howling down the river. If you can handle such a wind the fishing can be very productive.

A 9 lb Hurunui brown.

TALES AND TECHNIQUES

The Hurunui is one of the best trout rivers in Canterbury. Being fed by Lake Sumner, it always has a reasonable flow and is not as prone to flooding as some Canterbury rivers. This makes it prime trout water as well as an important salmon fishery.

It was salmon that first brought me to the Hurunui. Peter Witteman had decided to try his hand at salmon-fishing. As I was going to be in Christchurch for the weekend, I readily accepted his invitation to join him. We would fish the Hurunui for the early salmon runs for which it is known.

This seemed like a good excuse to visit a tackle shop to buy some new gear. As I was unlikely to get much use out of a salmon rod in Auckland, I decided to invest in something that would be useful for sea-fishing as well (the wallet not quite stretching to a rod for every kind of fish). I settled on a newly developed graphite rod: the Albagraph 6. This was teamed up with an Abu bait-casting reel that had all sorts of fancy devices to prevent the spool overrunning — not all of which, unfortunately, proved idiot-proof. Despite tuition from both the shop and Pete, my first cast resulted in a spool full of overrun 7 kg nylon. I retreated to the bank and spent the next hour untangling the mess. Meanwhile Pete was giving the water above the main bridge a good going-over.

Having sorted out my mess, I rejoined the fray. Pete gave me a few pointers on how to get the lure tumbling along the bottom, and after a while I had the hang of it. I even managed to time the application of my thumb to the spool to stop any overrun. I imagine serious salmon-fishers are easily recognised by the big callous on one of their thumbs.

After an hour of casting, allowing the lure to sink, winding on the handle to retrieve it, swinging the rod behind and casting again, I was getting rather bored. It was about then that I recalled how Dave Bowron, of Christchurch woolskin tannery fame, had once told me why he had given up salmon fishing. He had worked out that he was averaging 2000 casts per salmon — a lot more effort than he ever spent on a trout. I was starting to see what he meant, and as my arm was getting tired, I retreated to the bank. Pete soon joined me and we discussed our options. While we were yarning, an older fisherman came up to us.

'How're you doing?' he asked.

'No good,' replied Pete. 'How about you?'

'I got a couple this morning but there'll be nothing moving now until dusk,' he confided.

'Why's that?' asked Pete.

'Well, the water's rather low and they won't move unless they have a bit of cover. If they can't get it from the water, they'll wait until it's a little less light.'

We chatted on for a while and discovered that Jim, as he was called, was averaging a couple of salmon per day. We knew that was pretty good, as no one else seemed to be catching fish at all.

After he had gone, Pete and I decided to chuck it in for the day and head back for a spot of sustenance. Later that evening, Jim came into the hotel with his wife. We bought them a beer, and the four of us ended up having dinner together. We discovered they were retired and living in a caravan in the camping ground just over the bridge. Jim told us that all they did all summer was follow the salmon. This meant spending the early season on the Hurunui, then heading down to the Rangitata, moving on to the Rakaia and ending up on the Waitaki. Jim confessed salmon-fishing was not his first preference, as he felt all salmon did when hooked was run downstream and shake their heads. He said he preferred fishing for trout as they fought a lot harder. Once the salmon season was over, he concentrated on trout for the rest of the year.

Two weeks later Pete met Jim again on the Hurunui, and Jim generously showed him his favourite salmon possie. He told Pete what to use and when to fish the pool, which turned out to be only just down the river from the main bridge. He said, with a smile, that he usually headed way downstream in case anyone was following him, before timing his arrival at the 'secret pool' just on dawn or dusk. Pete took two salmon from the pool that weekend and two the next, so Jim's advice was spot on.

It was interesting to have a yarn with such a well-travelled angler, and his comments on salmon-fishing persuaded us we might be better off chasing the not-quite-so-elusive trout. The next morning saw us negotiating the narrow winding road to Lake Sumner and the upper reaches of the Hurunui. Despite Pete taking it carefully, the drive was not incident-free; we managed to get clipped by a ute cutting a corner while heading the other way. Pete was not happy that his near-new company car had a ding in it, but at least he had the boss as a witness. Another twenty minutes saw us on the road above a deep gorge. Pete stopped the car and we scrambled down the cliff as far as we could safely go.

'Good grief!' exclaimed Pete. 'Look at those monsters.'

Swanning around in the security of the inaccessible pool were several very large trout.

We had a good look for a way down to the water, but without a very long rope a descent was impossible. Reluctantly we left the trout for the Edmund Hillary types and returned to the car.

We continued along the dusty road to where it veered away from the river. There was a gate on the right that went through some paddocks to a camping area. The river here was quite wide but fairly shallow. Having come equipped with lightweight waders and felt-soled wading boots, I volunteered to cross to what would be the best side for a left-handed caster.

It was a pretty treacherous crossing, even though the river was low. The rocks were like greasy bowling balls, generously coated with slime. The reason, of course, was the river was lake-fed and did not receive huge 'freshes' that flushed the algae from the rocks. This indicated the fishing would be good, as the water level didn't fluctuate hugely and there would be plenty of feed for nymphs to graze on. I slowly edged across the river, with plenty of comments on the wading ability of North Island anglers accompanying my progress. No doubt Pete knew very well what the crossing was like and had been delighted at the naivety of my offer.

Finally reaching the far side, I sat down to assess the fishing conditions. It wasn't going to be an easy stretch to fish, as there were few obvious obstructions to break up the wide, strong flow. The reach above me was almost entirely unbroken for several hundred metres, with only the odd protruding rock and the occasional segment of riffly water. I knew from the wade over that the bottom of the river had plenty of rocks to break the sub-surface flow and give a bottom-hugging trout respite from the current. The problem was, looking at the surface of the water it was impossible to determine where the trout might lie. Normally, some disruption of the surface indicates where the rocks are, even if they are completely submerged, but on the Hurunui there are few such indicators. And thanks to the speed of the current and the volume of water flowing down, it would be hard to spot trout. Even at the edges the river flowed strongly, so it would also be hard to see fish in the shallows.

I decided blind-nymphing would be the best approach. However, when faced with such a daunting expanse of water to prospect, it is essential to break the task up into bite-sized chunks. The best way of blind fishing big water is to use the 'shotgunning' technique. This is a methodical way of quartering the river to ensure you cover every possible lie. Realising I would have to keep my nymphs near the bottom, I tied on a reasonably heavy one, followed by a size 14 Hare'n'Copper Flashback. I positioned the small indicator at the top of a 3 m leader.

Shotgunning involves casting in a fan pattern to cover all the water in front of you. I like to stay on the bank at first and fish near the edge in case there are any browns lurking in the shallow, slightly slower water. Then I cast further and further out, towards the middle of the river. If it is possible to wade, I move out a few metres and complete another fan of casts.

When all the water has been completely covered, regain the bank, move up a few paces and repeat the process. Whenever you come across some change in the surface flow, it pays to give the area a real going-over. It may be a protruding rock, a riffly stretch, a glassy glide in the middle of a fast section, some broken white water, a darker looking line indicating deeper water beyond after a ledge — anything that indicates an underwater obstruction. Wherever a strong, even flow of water is interrupted is a good spot to fish hard.

Halfway up that long stretch, I was well into the rhythm of ten or so casts followed by a move into or up the river. It is very relaxing to settle into this methodical pattern, even if you are still concentrating on the drift of the fly. In many respects the technique is similar to downstream wet-lining, except you are going upstream, not down.

Casting in a fan pattern.

It was then I noticed a seam about 10 m out where the flow seemed slightly slower than nearer the bank. A couple of casts eventually resulted

5th
4th
3rd
2nd
1st cast

in a drift right down the seam. The indicator dipped as a large fish seized the nymph. It took some landing in the strong flow, but finally a 2.2 kg brown hen came to the bank. I briefly admired the well-defined dark spots on the lighter-coloured flanks before easing it back into the current. Pete had long since disappeared round the corner so I could not show him that the difficult wade had been worth the effort.

The shotgunning technique produced two more browns from that long stretch of water, and having taken two hours to work my way up, I felt I had thoroughly covered it. You could decide to fish more quickly and hap-hazardly, but you might easily end up with nothing to show for your efforts, having missed all the lies. By the end of the day, shotgunning had yielded five fish, which was a pretty good result for a day on the Hurunui.

Up until my last excursion on the Hurunui, I did not believe the river held many really large trout. However, a blustery December day in the Sisters Stream area changed that perception for good. A deep green pool and the riffle above it yielded five trout — a ten-pounder from the pool; then an eight-, five-, six-, and nine-pounder followed from the riffle. All

Pool on the Hurunui in the Sister's stream area.

took a small beadhead and the choice of fly was not critical. The howling nor'wester had disrupted the surface of the water to such an extent that the big fish were happy to leave the security of the deep pool to feed freely in the fast, shallow riffle. It was not possible to cast delicately, but the fish seemed undisturbed by the line being dumped heavily on the water as I battled with the wind. They had lost their usual caution and were feeding like there was no tomorrow. It might pay to consider fishing on such windy days if you want to have a better chance of a trophy-sized fish from this river.

One trip to the Hurunui was notable for a very different catch. Pete and I had been taking an English chemical technician around the country. Some overseas visitors can be hard work, but fortunately Kevin was blessed with a good dose of that famous North England sense of humour, so he fitted into Kiwiland well. It wasn't long before he was dubbed 'Kev the Pom' and invited to come fishing with us for the weekend. Pete's wife, Di, also joined us, and during the day's fishing in the lower reaches, she noticed there were a lot of mushrooms around. They looked delectable and Di was keen to take home a basketful. As neither Di nor I were early-morning people, it fell to Pete and Kev to rise at the crack of dawn to scout the fields bordering the river for fresh mushrooms.

The boys had little trouble collecting a heap of the delicacy. Kev was amazed at the size of the mushrooms — as big as dinner plates, he reckoned. (He reported later they also tasted great at dinner that night at Pete and Di's.) Having completed their duty, Pete and Kev focused their attention on the number of rabbits out and about in the early light. Pete had his .22 rifle and a shotgun in the car boot, so the two of them proceeded to waste a few of the pests to fill in the time before breakfast. Returning to the hotel, they proudly showed us their 'catch'.

It was thought this might be the only 'trophy' Kev would have to show for his weekend's efforts, so his salmon-fishing gear was dug out and it was down to the riverbank to have his catch recorded for posterity. The ensuing photo of Kev, proudly holding a salmon rod with a rabbit attached to a chrome salmon lure, still has pride of place on his mantelpiece today. Apparently, there are several versions of how the bunny came to be attached to the hook, the veracity of the story being proportional to the intake of Newcastle Brown Ale.

While fishing for rabbits may not be your thing, there is no doubt the Hurunui offers a good chance of catching some trout, or even a salmon, depending on your patience threshold. As mine is low, I'll continue to chase the plentiful browns in the upper reaches of this wonderful river. Only when I start to average 2000 casts per trout will it be time to consider bunny-fishing.

Rabbit fishing.

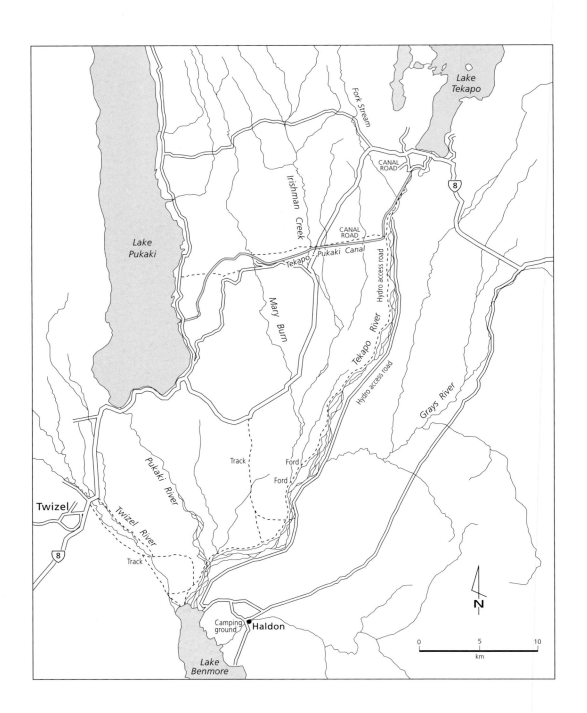

Tekapo River
Inducing the take

DESCRIPTION AND DIRECTIONS

The first sight of the Tekapo River can be a bit traumatic. There is plenty of water in the canal that transfers water from Lake Tekapo to Lake Pukaki, but this leaves only a trickle in the river itself below the Tekapo dam. There must have been many would-be anglers who have dismissed the dried-up riverbed as a serious trout river. That is true for the first few kilometres downstream from the dam, but roughly halfway along there is a considerable inflow from a number of tributaries: Irishman Creek, Fork Stream, Mary Burn on the west side, and Grays River on the east. Fishing is possible from the Fork confluence down. The only problem is getting here.

The only access to the true left bank is River Road, the old hydro-access road that starts below the dam just out of Tekapo village. 'Rough' does not begin to describe this route. It is not recommended for anyone who cares for their car. Unless you have a high clearance 4WD vehicle or similar, the large stones that form the road base will give the underneath of any saloon car a real pounding.

It takes around 45 minutes of slow driving to reach the Mary Burn confluence. But if you have the vehicle to cope, you will be rewarded by the sight of a delightful series of pools and riffles — not to mention a trout population of 250 fish/km. It is hard to believe this river, with its hugely fluctuating flow, could hold so many fish. However, drift/dive surveys have consistently confirmed these numbers. Presumably the fish run up from the huge body of water that is Lake Benmore, a few kilometres downstream.

River Road travels the entire length of the river, but the exit points at Pukaki and Twizel can be badly eroded and may be negotiable only by serious 4WD vehicles. It pays to check at the local service station whether these access points are navigable. If not, it is necessary to return to the Tekapo end to leave the river.

Access to the other side of the river is gained from the road to Haldon Arm on Lake Benmore. Grays River is crossed halfway down and the main river can be reached via the tributary. Further down it is possible to cross

the farm fields to the river if you have permission. At the end of Haldon Road is a good camping ground, a popular spot during the summer holidays. There are rough tracks up the river for some distance from here, but again 4WD is recommended — it's a long way to the nearest tow truck. There was an old bridge — the Iron Pot Bridge — across the river not far up from the camping ground, but at last report this was no longer in use.

The fishing is good from the mouth right up to the Fork Stream junction, but perhaps best around the Mary Burn confluence. The river can be easily crossed in normal flows in this area. Both rainbow and brown trout are present in huge numbers, with an average weight of about 1.4 kg. Bigger fish up to 4 kg are present, but they are more likely to be caught in the tributaries, such as the Mary Burn or Grays, as long as these have sufficient water. Outside of holiday periods the river is not subject to much pressure, and it's a great place to take a novice fly-fisher, as the fishing is easy. This, combined with the beauty of the surrounding mountains, can make for a magic day.

The Tekapo River road.

TALES AND TECHNIQUES

'Sorry, Mr Avis!' came the cry from the back seat once again as another large stone crashed into the underbody of our rental car.

'Yeah, yeah,' I said to Steve. 'Just be glad it's not your car.'

'Why didn't you hire a 4WD?' asked Bill.

'I tried to but they didn't have one available. Anyway, we're nearly there.'

As I manoeuvred round yet another boulder, the sight of the willows bordering the Mary Burn came into view. Another 100 m saw us edging over the wooden lining of the ford through the stream.

'See that pool up there under the willows?' I asked.

'Yeah,' replied Bill. 'What about it?'

'Last trip I got a nice five-pound brown out of there and a seven pounder a bit further up.'

'How come we never see your big fish, Gillies?' enquired Bill. 'You're always rambling on about these monsters you catch but you never bring one home.'

'That's why he's still there and probably going ten pounds by now,' I countered. 'If you stop moaning about the road, I might show you the pool later.'

That brought some respite as we drove down the road a couple of kilometres. I was looking for a long riffly pool I had fished on my first visit to the Tekapo, three years before. Once again I was indebted to Peter Witteman for telling me about the great fishing in this most unlikely location. Pete had told me he had started in at the lake end of the river and fished up for a whole day. Near the end of his day, he had really started to get into the fish, so he advised me to start in about one day's fishing up from the lake. I figured, for a fit guy like Pete, that would be around 10 km up, so I studied a map of the river. It seemed somewhere just down from the Mary Burn confluence would be about right. That's how I discovered the pool I now wanted to show the boys.

On that first visit, I waded across the river and wandered up the far bank looking for trout. I couldn't spot any, so I decided to warm up on a featureless stretch before tackling a good-looking riffle 30 m further up. I chucked out a few metres of line, prior to stripping off yet more ready to shoot through the rings. The indicator dipped, and an age later the message got through to a not-quite-ready brain that I had better do something. I lifted the rod and was straight into a feisty 1.5 kg rainbow. It seemed to be about as surprised as I was but soon recovered its senses and shot off down the pool. Five minutes later it was on the shingle, silver flank flashing in the sunlight.

Releasing it, I resumed where I had left off, a little more ready this time. Five fish later, I still hadn't reached the start of the riffle. Twenty fish and two hours later, I finally made it to the top of the pool — exhausted. The fish had been a mixture of browns and rainbows, most weighing around 1.4 kg. The biggest had been a 1.75 kg brown. Most had gulped the size 14 beadhead, while the odd stupid one had taken the size 12 sinker. The fish had all been in good condition and put up an energetic fight. I couldn't remember ever catching as many fish in such a short time — not even in the middle of a big run on the Tongariro River in the good old days.

Unfortunately, on this second visit the big pool was gone — partly because the river was now much lower, partly because it had swung over to our bank, leaving the old channel empty.

'Sorry boys, I'm afraid the pool's disappeared,' I said. 'You can see where it used to be over there.' I pointed to the dry channel.

'We're here now,' said Steve, pragmatic as ever, 'so we may as well get into it.'

'Yeah, sure,' I replied, 'but I'm just concerned there isn't enough water here. The fish may have dropped down the river.'

'Well, I for one have had quite enough of that road for a while,' said Bill. 'Let's give it a try.'

We untangled our rods from the mess in the boot and tackled up. Steve elected to stay on the near side while Bill and I crossed over. I gave Bill a couple of flies and made a few suggestions as to where trout might be lying in the pool upstream. Bill started in at the tail while I explored further up. However, an hour's fishing saw only a couple of small ones taken. I wandered back downstream to see how the others were doing.

'Jeez, Gillies, where's all the fish?' were the first words from Bill.

'Well, Speeds, I warned you it might be too low,' I replied.

A grunt was the only response.

I decided to have a look downstream. There were some good-looking riffles — quite different water from what the boys were fishing. Even though they looked a bit shallow and fast-moving, I decided to put a beadhead through one of them. Bang! The indicator stopped abruptly near the edge of the flow, in about 50 cm of water. A 2 kg rainbow dashed for the mess of dead tree limbs on the far side. It burrowed in and stayed there. I crossed the river and moved up to the jumble of driftwood. The fish was wedged under a large branch. It appeared to have got itself stuck, so I reached for the forceps and leaned down. A quick yank of the fly and the fish was free but still stuck. I lifted the branch and off it shot.

Steve had wandered down to see what was happening.

'Must have been the fastest-landed fish on record,' I said. 'Beached in ten seconds.'

'What, all one hundred grams of him?' came the response I should have expected.

Still, being a nice guy, I passed on the information that the fish might be lying in the riffles. It made sense, with the water being so low, that they would feel more comfortable in the ruffled water. It wasn't long before Steve was into his first Tekapo brown, a nice fish of about 1.4 kg. Selectively fishing the riffles saw us land several more of similar size. By the time we had to pack up for the drive to Queenstown, we had caught a total of ten fish, all but one or two taken from the shallow riffles. It wasn't quite the success of my earlier visit, but it had shown my companions the potential of the river. However, they weren't appreciative enough to restrain themselves from a further host of 'Sorry, Mr Avis' jokes on the rough ride back. Plus they awarded me the 'Dick of the Day' award for catching the most stupid fish in the river. It is definitely getting harder to find congenial fishing company.

The next visit to the Tekapo saw me driving down the other side to the Haldon Arm of Lake Benmore to check out the lower river. I had been told there was a bridge there and figured this might save me the tortuous journey down the hydro-access road. As I was in my own car, that route was not an attractive proposition. I reached the well-laid-out camping ground, which I imagined would be very popular with boaties in summer, and after negotiating a few dead ends, gained the river and found the 'bridge'.

What a sight! It looked as if the jib of a construction crane had been lowered across the river. The whole thing looked ready to fall into the water in the first decent nor'wester. I nosed the car up to the on-ramp and jumped out to take a look. There was a narrow plank on each side, just wide enough for a tyre to fit onto. It was hard to believe the bridge was still usable but the guy at the Tekapo garage had assured me it was fine. What's more, I didn't fancy the long drive back through Tekapo to the other side of the river.

Steve releases a
Tekapo brown.

The desire to fish conquered fear, and I gingerly edged the car up the ramp and onto the bridge. Concentrating on keeping the wheels on the narrow planks at least meant I didn't have the chance to look down. I finally reached the far side with nothing more than a sharply increased heart rate. There was no way I was going back over that contraption, so I was faced with a rocky drive up the access road. Sorry, Mr Subaru!

Driving up the road, I kept a lookout for likely water. The river was a lot bigger down here, with the pools more defined. Each time I saw a good stretch, I would stop and have a fish. There weren't the same numbers of trout as up nearer the Mary Burn, but enough to provide interest. The fishing was pretty easy, and the trout weren't fussy. Such occasions are rare, and a good time to try out alternative techniques. When you fish a river with only the occasional trout, you tend to stick to your most successful method, reasoning that it will give you the best chance of hooking a fish. But when there are plenty of fish, you can afford to experiment. Then, when you are having a hard day, you can delve into your bag of tricks and try something different.

One of the most effective alternatives is the 'induced' take. The best-known method is the one popularised by James Leisenring and known as the 'Leisenring lift'. The basis of this technique is to cast upstream at a 45

The Leisenring lift.

degree angle to give the weighted nymph time to sink to the bottom. Hold the rod parallel to the water and retrieve any loose line so you are directly connected to the fly. As the end of the line sweeps past you, lift the rod smoothly high into the air. It is essential to move your line hand up to near the first ring in anticipation of a strike, as you will not be able to lift the rod to strike in the normal way.

Lifting the rod draws the nymph from the bottom towards the surface, so imitating the rise to the surface of an emerging aquatic insect. The take, if it comes, will normally be during the rise of the nymph. If there is no take, lower the rod, gather the slack line and fish out the cast. The method works best in slower water, where trout might expect to see emerging nymphs swimming to the surface. In faster water it would be unnatural for a nymph to rise so firmly against a strong current.

As a final flourish (you can do this even with a normal dead drift), allow the line to swing round at the very end of the drift. The nymph will swing out of the faster water into the slower, at the edge of the river. At the same time it will rise, as the taut line drags it up. Although the nymph is no longer progressing downstream with the current, it is common to get a take at this point.

Ninety percent of takes will be from small fish that have not yet worked out that nymphs should not be rising against the flow of the current. However, just once in a while a good fish will seize the fly at this point. This will usually happen when you have left the line trailing in the water as you search your fly box for something more successful. You'll get a hell of a fright as the rod is nearly pulled from under your arm. For some reason, this seems to happen most frequently when more standard methods have brought little success. I have often fluked a good fish this way, in the middle of an otherwise blank day, and have found that continued use of the technique fetches another good fish or two, making for a reasonable tally.

Why this is, I am not too sure. It may be there is a lot of subsurface insect movement going on, even if no sign of this is visible on the surface. For whatever reason, trout on these days seem to prefer a rising nymph, even if the movement is not what might be considered entirely natural. Fortunately, we don't have to worry why this is, just use it to our advantage.

Other methods of inducing a take include those most often used in still water, such as hand-twist retrieves, imparting action to the fly using the rod tip, and any other means of giving movement to the nymph. If the standard dead drift is not working, they are all worth a try. After a few hours of fruitless fishing I always feel it is time to experiment, but it is an advantage to have practised a new technique before giving it a go in tough conditions. A river with plentiful trout, such as the Tekapo, is the ideal place to expand your repertoire. You need to know what you are doing right when a take occurs so you can repeat your success. If a new technique is not working on such a productive river, you know there is more work to be done to refine it.

All this makes for an interesting day, and it will be with a real sense of triumph that you pick up a few fish with a completely new technique. And, when there are 250 trout in every kilometre of water, you won't have to work very hard.

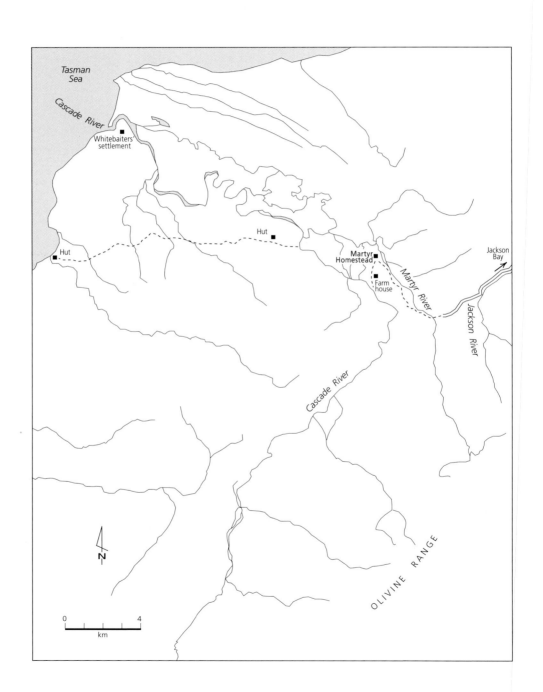

Tasman
Sea

Cascade River

Whitebaiters'
settlement

Hut

Hut

Martyr
Homestead

Farm
house

Jackson
Bay

Martyr River

Jackson River

Cascade River

OLIVINE RANGE

N

0   4

km

Cascade River
Reading the water

DESCRIPTION AND DIRECTIONS

The Cascade River is off the beaten track and must be one of the best-kept secrets in New Zealand. It has probably been fished by only a handful of anglers because of its location at the very end of the road down the West Coast of the South Island. Most travellers turn east at Haast, heading through the Haast Pass to the delights of Wanaka and Queenstown. Even the few intrepid souls who venture south beyond Haast probably only get as far as Jackson Bay. So it may come as a surprise to learn the road continues another 20 km from there, finally ending in the remote, wide

Whitebaiting settlement on the Cascade.

Cascade valley. It is 280 km from here down the coast to the next settlement.

The Cascade road is of a reasonable standard and doesn't usually require 4WD. It passes the Jackson River but, although attractive, this apparently holds few trout. The road narrows through Monkey Puzzle Gorge, but the drive is worth the view from the top of the ridge before descending to the river valley. On reaching the end of the road, it is necessary to ask for access permission from the farm owner at the new Martyr homestead.

Not far below the house is the crystal-clear Martyr River. This can be fished all the way down to its confluence with the Cascade. Brown trout up to 4 kg may be seen, with an average weight of around 1.75 kg. Most have the silver sheen of sea-run brown trout, no doubt brought into the river by the large whitebait runs. It is several kilometres down to the Cascade, and it would take a full day to fish this stretch thoroughly. The Martyr fish are surprisingly spooky, possibly owing to the clarity of the water and the lack of cover. The best approach is to have a spotter hidden in the matagouri on the high bank. This will allow you to stay well away from your quarry, while being guided to its lie by directions from the bank.

The area around the confluence fishes well at any time of the year. This is big water, and it isn't normally possible to wade to the far side, but there is good fishing in both directions from here. The many riffles and classic pools provide plenty of variety, with fish averaging around 1.5 kg. These are wild trout in superb condition, and strong leaders are required to subdue them in the heavy water. In the main river the trout take freely, especially to a beadhead fly fished through the faster flows.

Fishing upstream is possible for 2–3 km before a gorge is encountered and no further progress can be made up the true right bank. A jet-boat can penetrate a few kilometres beyond here, but even this is halted by the shallowness of the rapids. It is then a matter of tramping or forking out for helicopter transport. There was an old track between the Cascade and the upper Hollyford valley, but this is not used much now so might be hard to find. There is so much underfished water, however, that there is no real need to venture far past the gorge.

The Cascade is one of the best whitebait rivers on the West Coast, and there is quite a large settlement at the mouth during the whitebait season. This is well worth a visit if a jet-boat is available. The conditions the whitebaiters put up with while pursuing their little delicacy would not be tolerated by many. They are a hardy lot, the West Coasters.

TALES AND TECHNIQUES

I only learned of the existence of the remote Cascade through a local jet-boat operator, Maurice Nolan. As well as farming on the banks of the Okuru River, Maurice runs a jet-boat service up the local rivers. I had hired him to run me up the Okuru, drop me off and pick me up several hours later. That expedition had not been very successful, as the river was still high from recent floods. That is the inherent problem when fishing the West Coast: the rivers are more often in flood than they are fishable.

On hearing of my relative lack of success, Maurice proposed we take off the next day and fish the Cascade. He explained he had good access to the river as he ran cattle on the farm in that valley. I had to look up the river in John Kent's *South Island Trout Fishing Guide*, as I had never heard of it. Fortunately it rated well so it didn't take me long to make a decision, especially when Maurice's all-in fee turned out to be much cheaper than what an average trout-fishing guide would charge for a day on a river.

At 8 o'clock the next morning, I met up with Maurice and his nephew, who came along for the ride. We crowded together in the cab of the ute and headed off down the road, jet-boat behind. On the way, Maurice expressed doubts about the chances of reaching our destination. He had heard that the recent heavy rain had washed out part of the road about halfway to the Cascade. Supposedly the local council digger was due there sometime that morning to carry out repairs.

We arrived at the spot to find a huge washout and no sign of the council worker. A small stream that was supposed to flow under the road through a culvert had poured across the top and washed away all but a metre or so of the formed surface. Rather than waiting around for official help, Maurice decided we should fill the gap ourselves. He reckoned the hole would be best plugged with a tree. Grabbing a chainsaw from the ute's toolbox, he climbed up the 10 m bank above the road, selected a dead 15 m beech at the edge and laid into it. It wasn't long before the tree toppled. However, instead of tumbling down the bank, it became caught up in the bush at the top and hung there, precariously balanced. Maurice couldn't get at the trunk to free it so scrambled back down.

The next idea was that we should fill the washout with the plentiful boulders lying on the side of the road. An hour of lugging these saw only a metre or so of the gaping hole filled, but Maurice reckoned that would do. Carefully, he edged ute and boat around the hole, right wheels on good road, left on the pile of rocks. Fortunately he made it. We climbed in

Middle Cascade.

and continued on our way. Such are the trials and tribulations of travelling on the Coast.

Half an hour later, we arrived at the bluff overlooking the Cascade valley. A stunning panorama lay below us. Far in the distance, the Cascade emerged from a narrow gorge, with the rugged Olivine Mountains beyond. Below the gorge, the river flowed across a flood plain several kilometres wide, created by the regular floods produced by the 1000 cm (400 inches) of rain the area receives every year. The wide valley was well grassed, and Maurice said his family had farmed it for several generations.

We drove down the hill to the end of the road and went through a farm gate. A short drive took us to a stunningly clear stream that meandered through the swampy paddocks. It was, Maurice informed me, the Martyr River. He also advised me to look carefully in the stream on the journey down.

We launched the boat and set off downstream. The clarity of the water was amazing. Maurice slowed the boat as we came to a deep corner pool, and a couple of trout, 3 kg plus, could be seen diving for cover. I looked longingly as these huge fish shot away. Maurice must have noticed and promised me a go at them on the return journey.

We continued on our way, reaching the Cascade a couple of kilometres further downstream. The pool at the confluence looked very 'fishy', but

Maurice counselled patience and careered up the river at full throttle. The boat seemed to have two speeds — dead slow or flat out. A short distance later, Maurice drove the boat onto a shingle bank on the true left bank. He said to tackle up — it was time to fish. What he didn't tell me was that above the shingle bank a shallow creek entered the river. We ploughed across the ankle-deep water and followed this 100 m up, Maurice refusing to give me any clues as to why we were doing so.

As we rounded a corner, I stopped dead, mouth agape. Ahead of us was a classic spring creek complete with unbelievably clear water and beds of waving weed. Even from 30 m away I could see a couple of dark shadows nosing around the weed. I looked down at my 6/7 weight river rod and thought wistfully about the 5 weight back at the hotel. The trout were feeding in water about 50 cm deep, so deceiving them would not be easy.

And so it proved. The strong wind blowing down the river valley made a delicate presentation difficult and accuracy nigh impossible. My first cast was deliberately short to give me some feel for the distance. It's usually a good idea to make the first cast short of your target to get an idea of how the wind might affect a serious effort. So much for theory. As I lengthened the cast to put the fly a metre above the fish, a strong gust deposited the whole lot on its head. Both trout shot into the weed beds. Maurice said nothing but I sensed his unspoken, 'Here we go again — another one who can't cast.'

I gathered in my loops of line and, without a word, moved on up. Maurice strode on ahead to spot for me. He didn't have Polaroids on so I wasn't too sure how successful he would be, but it turned out he had an uncanny ability. He would point to something in the stream, and after I had stared hard for a while, I would finally see the trout he had spotted. In all my years of trout-fishing, I have met only one person who was a match for Maurice when it came to spotting, and he was a guide who did it for a living, armed with an expensive pair of Polaroids.

My casting did not improve. The banks were now clad with thorny matagouri, and between catching the line on the thorns and having it blown around by the wind, I was getting embarrassed. Maurice carried on, full of encouragement (despite what he was probably thinking), before stopping at a pool surrounded by matagouri trees so large they met above the water. It looked impossible to fish. Swanning around in this sylvan seclusion, free of care, was a large trout — the biggest we had seen so far. Sighing inwardly at the likelihood of another failure, I pulled out some line and crept to the tail of the pool.

An abbreviated reverse roll cast was my only hope of getting a fly near the trout. Fortunately the bush was now sheltering me from the worst of the wind and my first attempt saw the size 14 Pheasant Tail plop in a metre above my quarry. A sheer fluke, but no one was to know. The little plop seemed to get the fish's attention: maybe it thought something had been blown into the water from the bushes above. It finned over quietly, and there was the flash of white as its mouth opened. I tightened gently to a satisfying stop as the hook bit home. For me, that's what trout-fishing is all about — that exhilarating moment when you have successfully fooled the wary trout. Even losing the fish cannot detract from the thrill of that moment.

And there seemed a good chance I would lose this fish, as it used every dirty tactic in the book to try to shed the hook. Luck was with me this time, though, and eventually a 2.5 kg brown jack came to the net. I was relieved and also redeemed when Maurice said the fish was the best they had caught in the spring creek for quite a while.

We proceeded back to the boat, and as we reached the main river we were surprised to see someone wading across towards us, waving frantic-ally. I briefly wondered if it might be a keen local ranger but couldn't imag-ine any ranger risking being swept away just to check on a licence. It turned out to be a tramper who wanted to know if we'd spotted his mates upriver. They were traversing the mountains from Wanaka via Mt Aspiring and were due any day.

The tramper introduced himself as Chris Earl, and being a rugby fan I recognised him as the recently retired Canterbury prop and brother of famous All Black 'enforcer' Andy Earl. Maurice invited Chris to join the party, probably fearing another crossing might be one too many, despite the obvious power of Chris's tree-trunk legs. It later turned out to be an invitation Chris should have declined. We all piled into the boat and raced upstream.

What a stunning trip. The valley narrowed now, and the beech-clad banks were mirrored in the still water of the large pools. The colour was indescribable, a turquoise/aquamarine I knew the camera would be unable to capture truthfully. I hoped there were a few spare neurons in my brain, sufficient to keep it in my memory banks for a year or two. Maurice took the jet-boat up as far as he could safely navigate and parked once more on the shingle. I took off upriver while the others put on the billy.

Above a nearby pool was a good-looking riffle crying out to be fished. I was probably the first to fish it for a year, if not the first ever. And I love

Fishing the seam.

fishing riffles. The broken water gives you some cover from a wary trout, as its window on the world above is disturbed. With no cover from tree or bank, you need this advantage. Riffle water is interesting to fish as well. You have to get the drift just right to match the current. The best attack is to fish the seam, where the fast mid-channel current meets the slower water at the edge.

Fish sit in the slower water ready to nip out into the faster flow to pick up any morsel of food rushing past. Like trout sitting in pocket water, they need to be quick because the food will be past in an instant. This gives the angler a further advantage, in that a fish doesn't have much time to inspect your offering. So there is no great need to match the hatch — just use a good-looking fly and get the drift right.

I waded out through the strong current to get within casting range of the riffle. On my second cast the indicator stopped abruptly and a 2 kg trout exploded from the water. It screamed over to the far side of the river, then raced upstream. I was well down into the backing, trying to retrieve line from the water to get in more direct contact with the fish. Fortunately it quietened down and gave me the chance to do this, and I was soon able to apply some sidestrain and gradually ease the trout back over to my side. A couple of runs later and a gleaming silver fish lay in the shallows at my feet. I admired the contrast of the distinct dark spots against the silver body for a couple of seconds before reaching down and freeing the fly.

Wading back out, I cast just above where I had started. Bang! Another brown exploded from the riffle, cartwheeling in its efforts to free the fly.

Having failed, it shot off down the riffle to the shallow tail of the pool, with me stumbling along trying frantically to regain some line. Down through the long rapids it went, my spool emptying at an alarming rate, then into the next pool, to jeers from the boys on the bank, cans in hand. Fortunately I was rapidly dragged past them by the fury of my fish. The power of these wild Cascade browns was mind-boggling: they fought more like a big Mohaka rainbow.

My headlong charge finally slowed as the fish ran out of puff, with heavily panting angler in the same state. I bulldozed it forcefully to the edge, taking advantage of the temporary respite before it regained its breath. The possible mate of the first fish was at my feet — a silvery 2 kg hen. The boys gathered round, their comments a tad more respectful than a few minutes earlier.

After freeing the fish, I looked at the long walk and wade back to the riffle. Then I looked at the cold can being proffered by Maurice. I decided the trout could spare me for a while. Lunch was spread out on the bow of the jet-boat and I tucked in, not realising how hungry I had become. My appetite had been suppressed by the distraction of the great fishing.

Half an hour later it was time to set off, and down the river we went at the inevitable full throttle. Maurice wanted to show me a side stream below the Martyr, so we steamed past the confluence, showering gravel and water in equal measure onto the banks of each corner. Not far down, a small stream edged quietly into the main flow. Maurice nosed the jet into the mouth and proceeded carefully up this 2 m wide creek. There was evidence of a recent major flood, with logs and branches littering both banks, and there were a couple of ominous clunks as we hit sunken obstructions.

Conditions became so bad Maurice decided to turn back. As he was trying to swing the jet-boat around, it lodged on a log under the surface. A burst of 375 Chevy failed to lift us off the obstacle. Chris said he would push us off and jumped in over the side. What he had failed to appreciate was the depth of the water, and his feet reached the bottom as the water reached his neck. A few expletives rent the chilly air as the impact of the glacial water hit him, but being the hard man he was he put his shoulder to the hull. More cursing followed as he struggled to dislodge several hundred kilos of boat and crew. Finally all those years in the scrum paid off and we scraped free. We hauled Chris aboard, blood pouring down his leg from a cut from a sharp rock. He was freezing cold. I dug out my Swanni and wrapped it round his shoulders, but he was still shivering badly. We quickly decided to curtail the fishing and get Chris back to his car and the warm clothes in his pack. This was accomplished in record time, with motor howling at full throttle. In dry gear in front of the car heater, Chris made a quick recovery.

I did have some fleeting regrets as we scattered large trout before us on the way back up the Martyr, but I figured the fish would keep. After all, it would probably be a year before they saw another angler. For anglers who like their rivers pristine, the Cascade offers a unique experience.

Canterbury props are tough.

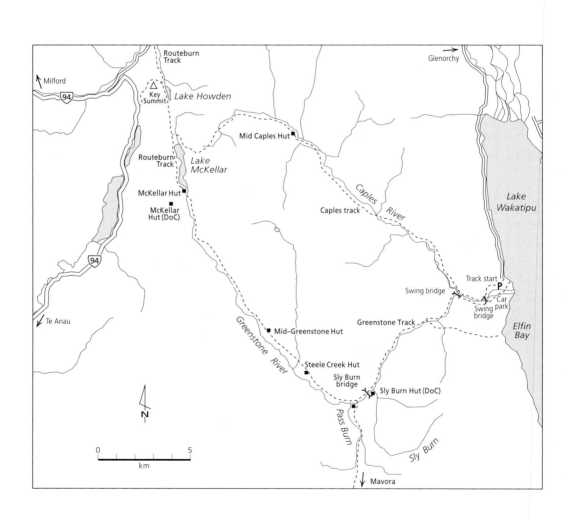

Greenstone River
Windy-day tactics

DESCRIPTION AND DIRECTIONS

The Greenstone River has its source in the cool waters of the beautiful Lake McKellar, alongside the Greenstone Track. The world famous walkway provides the only access to the river, and to fish the better water requires an overnight stay. Fortunately there are several well-appointed huts, both public (DoC) and private. The private huts belong to the Routeburn Walk Company, which takes regular guided tramps up the Greenstone between November and April (depending on the weather).

The track starts close to where the river spills into Lake Wakatipu, just north of Elfin Bay, along the western shore. Overland access to this point involves a long 86 km drive from Queenstown round the top of the lake through Glenorchy and Kinloch, passing over the Rees and Dart rivers. Quicker access is by water taxi direct from Queenstown, as the Greenstone lies on the opposite side of the lake from Queenstown. The car park at the end of the road marks the start of the Greenstone and Caples tracks.

It is possible to fish the lower pools up from the mouth, but these receive a lot of pressure from boat-based anglers. Accordingly, it is better to head up the track for about an hour to the confluence of the Greenstone and Caples rivers. There is good fishing both above and below here. The track crosses the Greenstone at this point and heads up the river through a steep gorge. There are fish in the gorge, but it is hard work clambering over the boulders, with generally only rather small fish in the pockets between the big rock slabs.

Above the gorge, near Slip Flat, is a short valley with some good pools, but this stretch rarely seems to hold a lot of fish. There is better fishing in the middle reaches about an hour up from the Mid-Greenstone or Steele Creek huts. Here the river opens out into a wide valley, hemmed in on both sides by beech trees. The track veers away from the river and continues through the forest, but it is easy going up the river itself for the 10 km to where it emerges from the bush at the top of the valley. The track can be found again at this point, and the two McKellar huts (one public, one private) are only a few minutes away. From here, it is a three-hour walk via the Divide to the Hollyford Road and transport to Te Anau.

The fishing in the valley can only be described as superb. The clear, green water of this wilderness river always attracts good numbers of fish from the lake. It is best fished early or late in the season, when the rainbows are running up to spawn, but it holds fish throughout the year, rainbows predominating. They average around 1.9 kg, but fish of up to 4 kg are there to be caught. Usually there is at least one fish in every pool, but after the heavy early-season pressure, they get very spooky and a cautious approach is essential. The pools are close together, with fast, bubbly rapids in between. Wading across the shallow tails is easy, as the clean gravel bed is free of slime. Unless it is abnormally hot, fish lie in the body of the pool and can be easily spotted. However, the tussock country doesn't provide much cover so a low profile is required — trouser kneepads are handy.

This is true wilderness trout-fishing, and catch-and-release should be considered mandatory to protect the fragile waterway.

TALES AND TECHNIQUES

There are few rivers in New Zealand more beautiful than the exquisite Greenstone. It is as though the river has taken the colour of the jade gemstone after which it is named. The river itself isn't actually a source of greenstone, or pounamu, but was used by early Maori as a route to the West Coast, where that treasured material was to be found. The Greenstone and Hollyford valleys provided the easiest passage from Central Otago to the west. The Greenstone valley is wide and open, passing through tussock flats, and is easy going compared with neighbouring valleys such as the Routeburn. This means the tramp in to the best fishing waters is not too strenuous, although an overnight stay is necessary to fish the river's middle reaches.

The first time I fished the Greenstone, the usual tramping team — Sue, Helen, Paul and I — did a day walk to check if the track was as good as the advertising blurb claimed. As it turned out, mere words could not do justice to the stunning beauty of the river valley. We took off early from Queenstown on the long drive round the top of Lake Wakatipu to the start of the track. In those days, the road to Glenorchy was unsealed and it was an arduous, dusty haul, especially if you got caught in the hordes coming back from the Glenorchy Races. However, the road has now been

The upper Greenstone. PHOTO COURTESY OF THE ROUTEBURN WALK COMPANY.

completely tarsealed all the way and makes an interesting drive, most of it along the lake edge. From Kinloch on, the road is rather narrow and winding, so take care, particularly as the buses carrying trampers to the start of the track tend to take up more than half the width of the road.

Arriving at the road end, we shrugged on daypacks and headed up the track. It wasn't long before we got our first sight of the river. The colour of the water was indescribable: the deepest, clearest green you could possibly imagine would not match what we saw looking down from the first swing bridge. And lying deep in the pool above the bridge was a big rainbow. Rod hands twitched as we peered down, but the object of our attention seemed unconcerned. Reluctantly we moved on, as there was just no way down to the pool — the fact of which the fish seemed fully aware.

About an hour's walk brought us to the junction of the Caples and Greenstone rivers. From the cliff above the junction pool we could see two large trout holding in deep water in the middle. However, while we were watching them, a party of trampers crossed over the Caples and came down to the pool. They shed packs and, to our surprise, outer garments too and proceeded to plunge into the river. Screams soon followed as the icy mountain water numbed sensitive regions. A mad scramble out ensued for all but a couple of hardy types. Naturally the trout had disappeared as soon as the first white body had invaded their domain. We figured they must be fairly spooky fish if this plunge-pool caper was a must for all track-walkers.

We continued over the Greenstone swing bridge and up through the beech-clad banks overlooking the steep gorge. There were a number of short, sharp pools here, but I had been told not to bother with these as they usually held only small fish. Beyond the gorge, the valley opened up in the Slip Flat area, and it was here the girls enjoyed a sunbathe while the boys had a fish.

The pool right in front of us looked very appealing so we went down to have a look. A good trout was feeding actively at the head. I managed to get a couple of reasonable drifts past it but they evoked no response. The next cast was dumped by a downstream gust of wind rather heavily on the placid water, and off the fish went. Shouts of derision followed from the sunbathers, who had witnessed it all, thanks to the clarity of the water.

We decided to move away from the audience that obviously had no appreciation of the finer points of fly-fishing. Unfortunately, that was the only decent trout we saw in the two hours we took to work our way through the short valley. We took a few small fish blind-nymphing the deeper runs, but that was it for the day. Still, we had seen some good ones earlier on, and we now knew the glowing descriptions we'd heard of the valley were no exaggeration.

A couple of years later, the same team was back at the start of the track, this time in pouring rain and with somewhat heavier packs. A plastic rod case poked out from the top of mine. A four-piece 5/6 weight 2.75 m rod was my choice for the trip. I also had a reel with a dull-coloured WF5F line and a spare spool with a brighter WF6F line for windy and/or rainy days.

As the first day required a long tramp, it wasn't until the second that we had the chance to fish. By then, Liam, the head guide, had taken note of our twitching rod hands and reckoned our withdrawal symptoms were getting serious. He volunteered to guide us down from the track to the river and accompany us up the valley. It turned out that the main reason for this generous offer was that he was a keen amateur photographer and wanted to add to his portfolio of fly-fishing photos.

One hour up from Steele Creek Hut, we farewelled the rest of the party and slipped through the beech trees down to the river. Tackling up, we advanced to the first pool. While we stood there, a ring appeared halfway up, near the far bank. On went a size 14 Kakahi Queen dry, and I cast a metre or so above the fish. It moved over and took a good look, slipping back down with the current as it inspected my offering. The fly must have withstood the detailed examination because it suddenly disappeared in a swirl. For a change I remembered to count to three and lifted the rod on three. The trout shot up the pool and jumped a metre out of the water. The impact from the landing threw the hook and the line came back to me. Perhaps I had counted too fast? Anyway, it was nice to have at least hooked my first decent Greenstone fish — rainbow of around 1.75 kg. We fished on, alternating pools but saw only two more trout in the couple of hours at our disposal before we had to move on to catch up with the rest of the group.

That night, the size of the lost trout was a popular topic as we relaxed over a glass or two of Country Dry White cask wine. It may not have been the best wine ever made, but after eight hours' tramping it tasted pretty good. Of course, the lost trout grew considerably with each retelling of the tale and each additional glass of wine. Unfortunately for me, Sue and I had instituted a 'Twit of the Day' award on the first night of the trek to liven up the daily pre-dinner drinks session. This backfired on me when I was the first nomination for losing such a huge fish. Fortunately, there had been far worse misdemeanours than mine that day, but we were warned to produce a fish the next day or face the consequences.

We rose early, and as it was a rest day, Paul and I were able to fish all day. We set off from the McKellar Hut and walked through the beech trees down to the start of the valley. The wind we had heard rustling the trees above was now whistling around our ears. A 50-knot southerly was howling down the valley. I had taken my 6 weight line, but even that looked rather inadequate in the face of the gale. Still, this was the only fishing day we were going to get. At least we would not have to put up with sunbathing onlookers.

Down the valley we went, to where we had started the day before. On the way down, we spotted several fish and marked them for our return journey. It seemed most pools had at least one in them. The water was clear and the pools were deep, with plenty of cover. Short rapids separated the pools, and wading was easy across the shallow tails. We had only our tramping boots for footwear, but they were fine on the clean gravel; felt soles were not necessary.

We soon found fishing into the teeth of the southerly was impossible. It was necessary to wait for a momentary lull in the gusting wind, then quickly throw out a few metres of line. The impossibility of casting a longer line produced another problem. We would see a fish lying in the body of a pool but had to get within 4 or 5 m of it, as that was the maximum we could cast. But from that close, as soon as the rod was waved, the trout took off.

To overcome the problem, I tried my old favourite — the from-the-current cast. However, the necessity of driving the rod strongly forward into the gale resulted in the line falling heavily on the water, and again off went the fish. Very frustrating. We tried blind-nymphing the deeper pools, but the trout were not holding deep. There were no riffles to hide a poorly cast line, the water consisting solely of pools with shallow rapids in between.

Despite spotting over 30 fish, we caught zilch. A very disappointing day. Needless to say we were unanimous joint winners of the 'Twit of the Day' award. Getting 'skunked' on a river was not a new experience, but one always likes to learn from it to avoid having it happen too often.

That night, a young guy came over from the DoC hut. He had been employed by the department to conduct a survey on anglers fishing the Greenstone. We had in fact seen him in the distance earlier in the day, fishing downstream from us. We asked him how he had got on, hoping he had encountered similar problems. He informed us, with a quiet smile, that he had taken five fish. We were astonished. Even though he knew the river well, having fished it virtually every day for three months, it was still surprising how well he had managed to cope with the wind.

On being questioned about this, he admitted there was a special technique involved. What he did was sneak to the head of a pool and chuck any old sort of cast into the fast water. He then let the current straighten out the wind-tossed mess. Mending downstream, he allowed the nymph to drift down the centre of the pool. If it was a long pool, with some concealment, he crept down it, moving at the same speed as his line. Reasonably close contact had to be kept with the fly as it entered the likely fish-holding area, as a take was more difficult to detect at this downstream angle. The fish, unspooked by rod, line or angler, accepted the nymph gratefully and the fight was on.

Our friendly angler admitted it was impossible to fish all pools like this, as in some the current was too fast or the lie too far down. But he believed it was the only way you could fish for such wary trout when the wind was howling down the valley. We were duly enlightened and only wished we had met our new friend the night before and thus avoided a frustrating day on the water. Still, we had learned something from our troubles and would be better prepared the next time we encountered the same conditions.

Greenstone technique – walking a cast down the pool.

Initial cast

current

Later that month, I was yarning in my local tackle shop with a near neighbour, Hamish Murray. Hamish had been in the New Zealand fly-fishing team for two years by then and had been our top angler at the previous year's world championships. I asked him if he had ever used the 'Greenstone technique' on a windy day. He was delighted to inform me he had. On the very same day we had been struggling on the Greenstone, he had been having the same problem on the upper Taieri River in Otago. His Otago fishing mate had then shown him the exact same technique I have described. Hamish said he had since had the chance to perfect it and had found it to be deadly efficient on a windy day — even in the dreaded Canterbury nor'wester. It was some relief to find out I was not as ignorant as I had first thought. The technique must be a well-kept Otago secret that gives the locals a distinct advantage over visitors when the wind blows.

It was interesting to discuss other matters with the survey-taker. He was even more forthcoming after a glass of Country Dry White. He had interviewed every angler who had fished in the area from the season opening on November 1 up to January 3, when we were there. The total was only 60 anglers — an average of two per day. Certainly this was no huge number, and with the amount of water available did not represent a 'thrashing' of the river — although the survey included anglers only along the middle reaches, not those day-fishing lower down. Of course, it takes some effort to get to the middle part of the river, and it is necessary to stay overnight. The isolation is the main factor limiting the number of anglers.

The survey also revealed that anglers on the Greenstone River rated its beauty and isolation over the quality of the fishing. This was pretty much our own point of view, and maybe the finding confirmed that most anglers on the river were of the same opinion as that prince of angling writers Roderick Haig-Brown, when he wrote: 'Perhaps fishing for me is only an excuse to be near rivers. If so, I'm glad I thought of it.'

We were too.

Sunset on the Greenstone. PHOTO COURTESY OF THE ROUTEBURN WALK COMPANY.

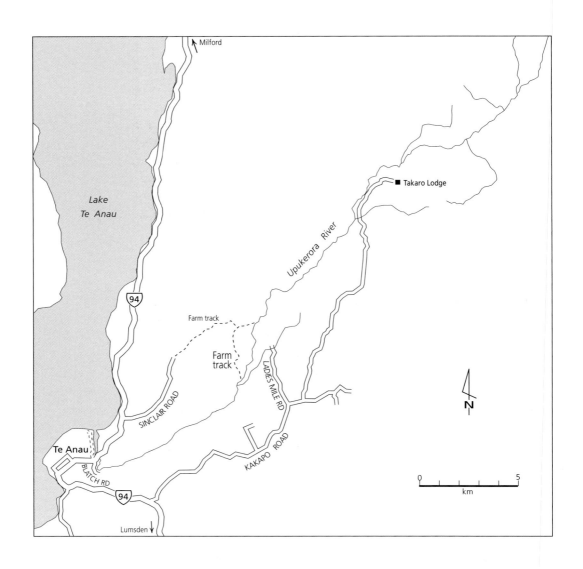

Milford

Lake
Te Anau

Takaro Lodge

Upukerora River

94

Farm track

Farm
track

SINCLAIR ROAD

LADIES MILE RD

KAKAPO ROAD

Te Anau

BLATCH RD

94

Lumsden

N

0   5
km

Upukerora River
Fishing the far bank

DESCRIPTION AND DIRECTIONS

The Upukerora River is one of those rivers often passed over by anglers on the way to fish supposedly more bountiful waters. Situated as it is on the doorstep of Te Anau, anglers heading off to the more famous Eglinton River probably give the Upukerora no more than a passing glance as they whiz over it just north of the township. Add to those the thousands who have tried and failed with the impossible Clinton River browns, and there are many that might have found catching a good fish a lot easier on the 'Upuk'. Admittedly, the river doesn't look too enticing at the highway bridge, but a kilometre or two upstream it improves dramatically.

The Upukerora starts its long journey deep in the heart of the Snowdon State Forest and flows south through beech forest until it emerges into farmland just below what was the Takaro Lodge. There is a gorge not far below the lodge, and from there down are many bubbly runs and delicate pools. However, most of the best water is further downstream still, and this can be accessed from Ladies Mile Road off Kakapo Road. Access to the area around the lower gorge is also available with permission from the farmers on the right of Sinclair Road. About halfway down to the lower gorge are some deeper pools near the old coal pit. In midsummer, when the river is low, this is the best section to try for a trout that may have postponed its return to Lake Te Anau.

The river is a major spawning stream for this huge lake, so holds most fish early or late in the season. They start moving upriver in April or May, which gives anglers a month or two before the season ends. Again, on the first day of the season, November 1, the river holds large numbers of trout averaging 1.5 kg, with plenty of larger fish present. The odd 4.5 kg trout has been caught, but generally 2.75 kg would be considered a good size for this river. The trout tend to drop back to the lake at the onslaught of summer, when the river flows decrease markedly. However, there are always a few resident fish wherever the water is deep enough to give them cover. The residents are a pretty even mix of rainbow and brown, but during the spawning season rainbows are predominant.

Below the lower gorge are some long pools with shingle banks that make for easy fishing and casting. All the pools have shallow tails, so wading is rarely more than ankle deep. This section can be reached from the end of Blatch Road. It takes a full day to fish from there up to the excellent water just above the lower gorge. This stretch is an interesting mix of runs, riffles, pools and glides, so there is water to suit every preference.

Below the bridge the river is different in character, the trout tending to lie under the overhanging willows on the far bank. This is a good spot to sneak out for an hour or two in the evening and drift a dry fly through the slower runs. After a kilometre or two, the river runs into the cold waters of Lake Te Anau, where most of the Upuk trout spend their summer. The mouth itself fishes well when the spawning trout are congregating, waiting for a fresh to spark the surge upstream.

TALES AND TECHNIQUES

The Upukerora is one of the most productive but least known rivers in all of the South Island. Perhaps the first man to recognise its potential was an American called Stockton Rush, when he built Takaro Lodge in the 1970s. The building caused quite a controversy at the time, as 'foreigners' were not allowed to own land in New Zealand in those days. Rush was given a special dispensation and built the 8,000 sq ft (743 sq m) lodge on a 1032 ha site on the upper Upukerora.

Takaro Lodge was one of the first establishments in New Zealand to target wealthy tourists seeking luxurious and exclusive accommodation at a unique wilderness location. Among early visitors was the famous American golfer Tom Weiskopf, who made quite an impact on the local browns. However, the project sparked such controversy that a new government reversed the original decision and the lodge was closed down.

Rush must have had some good advice on where to site his exclusive retreat, as locals swear that during the spawning run in those days you could count over 100 fish in each of the two big pools just downstream. Although Kakapo Road leads to the lodge, access is usually not allowed by the owners and the gate is generally padlocked. The lodge is being developed by the new owners into an exclusive health spa, so it is unlikely access will be granted for anglers wanting to fish the upper Upuk.

Even today, the river can yield large numbers of fish during the earliest part of the season. One of the local farmers has a nephew who visits it every year for the first week, from 1 November. This angler is also an honorary fishing ranger and, naturally, a fervent believer in catch-and-release. The farmer told me how, a couple of years ago, the nephew and a fishing mate had landed 199 fish in just ten days and wanted just one more fish to complete their double century.

The farmer related how he'd pointed out a good fish lying in the tail of a pool immediately downstream.

'Nah,' said the nephew, 'we caught him this morning. We need a fresh one for our two hundredth.'

The three of them moved up to the next pool, where the nephew spotted and hooked a nice 2 kg rainbow.

'Here you are, Harry,' he said, proffering the arched rod and attached fish to his uncle. 'You're always complaining you've never caught a trout on a fly rod — land this one for us.'

The rod was snatched from his hand before he might reconsider this generous offer. Despite his lack of familiarity with the tackle, the farmer landed the 2 kg fish before returning it to the river. That evening, over a few celebratory drinks, he was regaling an audience with the tale of his big catch. His nephew pulled out something from his pocket and leaned over.

'Here's something so you can remember the fish,' he said, presenting a piece of paper to the farmer.

'What is it?' asked the farmer, trying to decipher the official-looking document.

'It's a ticket for fishing without a licence,' replied his nephew, and the two fishermen collapsed with laughter.

The farmer read the details on the offence notice while the anglers cackled away about putting one over the older man.

'It says here that the tackle I used is confiscated too. Where should I hand in your rod?' he asked, his face deadpan. There was a moment's silence before the nephew realised he had met his match. The offence notice was quickly retrieved and ripped up — somewhat earlier than may have been the original intention, reckoned my farmer friend.

As with the anglers in the story, there is a good chance that if you can be on the river early or late in the season, you will have a field day. I was lucky one March to arrive as the river was clearing after two days of heavy rain. It had been low for many weeks, and even now it was still rather thin-looking. I wasn't sure the fish would have enough cover. A local farmworker confirmed my suspicion and told me he had never seen the river so low in the twenty years he had been living in the area. He was somewhat doubtful of my chances of even finding a fish but suggested I head down to near the coal pit, where the pools were a bit deeper.

Tackling up, I prepared for a day fishing shallow water. This meant a 5 weight rod, a subdued olive-green fly line and a long, fine-tapered fluorocarbon leader. As I checked out the water on the way down, it didn't look promising. I resolved to concentrate on the riffles, where the trout might have more cover than the shallow, clear pools could offer. This meant a small indicator would be useful, so on went a 1 cm snippet of yarn about a metre up from the fly. The indicator also helped to show where the line was, as the olive colour can be hard to see in poor light conditions. As I would be prospecting, I put on the usual double-fly rig of a lightly weighted size 12 Caddis and a size 14 unweighted beadhead Hare'n'Copper. The farmer had suggested this pattern might be the most productive.

The first pool in the coal-pit area yielded a slabby 1.2 kg rainbow, and I thought this would probably be a typical fish for the day. Above the pools was a riffle that looked deep enough to shelter a trout, and I threw an exploratory cast up the middle, albeit without much expectation. There was time for only a couple of metres of drift before the nymph was seized with a violent take. A small one, I thought, as little fish always seem to take more fiercely than big ones. But a strong 2.5 kg silver-sided rainbow exploded from the water to dispel that particular theory. It raced up and down the riffle with amazing speed. No way was this some weak resident recovering from a long, dry summer. Eventually the fish started to tire and I was able to bring it into the shallows. What a delightful surprise on a day when not too much had been expected. I unhooked the beadhead Green Caddis, and the jack quickly swam off downstream.

Recasting a little bit further up the riffle, I was astonished when the small yarn indicator dipped again and a 1.5 kg brown surged up the pool. A few circuits later she was duly landed, with the Hare'n'Copper beadhead tail fly embedded in her jaw. Three fish in one hour — this was exciting stuff!

The next few hundred metres of river proved too low — a few exploratory casts in the most likely runs, no more than 50 cm deep, yielded nothing — and there were no pools in which trout could be sheltering. I decided to head back to the car and drive down to near the lower gorge, where I had fished before. Half an hour later, I had driven through the farm and walked across the upper terrace paddocks to the river. Starting in just above the gorge, I quietly approached a deep pool that had fast water at

the top and a lovely slow glide, its deep-green water reflecting the bush above. Peering in, I saw the shadow of a reasonable-sized fish. A cast a metre above was rewarded by another fierce take. These fish were hungry! A 1.5 kg silvery rainbow was duly landed, and a further four identical fish followed in the next hour. It was obvious the rain and cold of the last few days had sparked a small run of maiden spawners. For a change, I was in the right place at the right time.

Coal Pit pool, middle Upukerora.

The fish took too strongly to be residents, as these would have tended to inspect their food more closely and been more judicious about what they took. However, the running fish would have been spooked by heavy lines and leaden flies splashing into the shallow pools or riffles. My stealthy approach and light gear saw them take with gusto, which made a pleasant change from the usually super wary southern trout.

The lack of caution on the part of these trout may have been partly due to the fact that the Upuk is not subject to a lot of fishing pressure. Outside of the first and last few weeks of the season, it is rare to encounter another angler there. I have done so only once, on my very first visit. It was a warm mid-January day, and I was fishing the delightful water above the lower gorge. Peering intently into a likely run, I was startled by a hail from an angler emerging from the scrub on the far side. We chatted for a while and it seemed we were having much the same success, having each landed two or three. He was an American, and I was interested to note that even during the heat of the day he was wearing long trousers. Commenting on this, he was pleased to inform me that at the end of the day his legs would be free of sandfly bites, matagouri scratches and rock grazes, whereas mine, clad in traditional Kiwi shorts, would have all the aforementioned and sunburn as well.

At the end of the day, when I surveyed my bitten, scratched and sunburnt legs, I resolved to wear long trousers from then on. A light woollen pair of old work pants was converted for the purpose, since when the only suffering at the end of a day's fishing has been from tired muscles. In recent years, the advent of polar-fleece fishing trousers has been a big improvement, as these have many advantages over the more common shorts and polypropylene — particularly when walking through the dreaded matagouri (or North Island gorse and blackberry).

The American also generously passed on the tip that the worthwhile fish were to be found lying hard against the far bank. They were spooked if you walked along that side, as the vibrations from your steps, sensed through their lateral line, warned them of your presence. A better approach, he suggested, was to stay on the open side and cast across to the slower water, right by the bank. This made a lot of sense, as I had

Fishing the far bank.

already spooked a fish while walking along a bank above a pool.

The next run up, I cast across the dividing ripple, aiming for the far side. Unfortunately, just as I cast, a gust of wind blew the Cicada dry fly out into the middle of the riffle. As I was about to retrieve this mess, a good-sized fish rushed out from beside the bank, chased the Cicada down the riffle and slashed madly at it. There was a great splash as it missed its target in the choppy waters. It wouldn't have made much difference if it had caught the fly, though, as I was standing there, mouth agape, trying to take in the drama, and would surely have missed the strike anyway. The next pool saw a better cast and a good 2.5 kg brown intercepted the bottom nymph as it drifted a few centimetres out from the bank.

Since that day, fishing the far bank has always proven a successful technique for me on medium-sized rivers. Your profile is low, and the faster water between you and the fish means less chance of being seen.

current

Mending.

The critical factor is to ensure the faster centre current does not drag the line downstream faster than the fly, which is in the slower water towards the edge. The way to prevent this is to mend the middle part of your line upstream. The faster the water, the more mending required.

You can also avoid drag by lifting the line out of the centre current. With your arm extended, you have maybe 4 m of reach, which is usually sufficient for a small or medium-sized river.

It is possible to fish the far bank on a larger river, such as the upper Mataura, so long as the current is reasonably even across its width. In slower water of this kind, you will often be able to spot your fish as it feeds, and mending the line might disturb the water and scare it. It is safer to cast just above the fish and not worry about mending. So long as the flow is even, drag won't be a problem. If the centre current is only slightly faster than along the far bank, you can try an S-cast, leaving some slack S-bends in the middle to absorb the extra flow. On big, fast waters, such as the upper Mohaka, no amount of mending or S-casts will be sufficient to slow the line to the speed of the far current, but on medium-sized rivers like the Upukerora, it is one of the most effective techniques of all.

There is no doubt that whenever you fish the Upukerora River, you will have a good chance of picking up a few fish, and occasionally you will catch a lot of fish. Lake Te Anau is New Zealand's second-largest lake, containing a huge number of trout, and at any time of the year some of these are running up the main spawning stream. So next time you're in Te Anau, give the Upuk a try — it's the South Island's Tongariro, and a lot more pleasant to fish.

# Bibliography

Borger, Gary A. *Nymphing.* Stackpole Books, Harrisburg, 1979.

Brook, Charles E. *Nymph Fishing for Larger Trout.* Crown Publishers, New York, 1976.

Busch, Tony. *Trout Fishing.* David Bateman Ltd, Auckland, 1994.

Gierach, John. *Fly Fishing Small Streams.* Stackpole Books, Harrisburg, 1989.

Haig-Brown, Roderick. *A River Never Sleeps.* Andre Deutsch Ltd, London, 1946.

Hill, Les and Graeme Marshall. *Stalking Trout.* The Halcyon Press, Auckland, 1985.

Hughes, Dave. *Reading the Water.* Stackpole Books, Harrisburg, 1988.

Kent, John. *North Island Trout Fishing Guide.* Reed Books, Auckland, 1989.

Kent, John. *South Island Trout Fishing Guide.* Reed Books, Auckland, 1990.

Kyte, Al. *Fly Fishing.* Leisure Press, Champaign, 1987.

Marsh, Norman. *Trout Stream Insects of New Zealand.* Millwood Press, Wellington, 1983.

McDowall, R.M. *New Zealand Freshwater Fishes.* Heinemann Reed, Auckland, 1978.

McKenzie, D.W. (ed.) *Reed New Zealand Atlas.* Reed Books, Auckland, 1997.

Orman, Tony. *The Sport in Fishing.* A.H. & A.W. Reed, Wellington, 1979.

Orman, Tony. *Trout with Nymph.* Hodder & Stoughton, Auckland, 1974.

Parsons, John. *Parsons' Passion.* The Halcyon Press, Auckland, 1990.

Roberts, John. *Illustrated Dictionary of Trout Flies.* Collins Willow, London, 1995.

Salmon, J.T. *The Native Trees of New Zealand.* A.H. & A.W. Reed Ltd, Wellington, 1980.

Sawyer, Frank. *Nymphs and the Trout.* A & C Black (Publishers) Ltd, London, 1958.

Schwiebert, Ernest. *Nymphs.* Winchester Press, New York, 1973.

Walker, Alf. *Fly Fishing Techniques.* Pagurian Press Ltd, Toronto, 1975.

Walker, C.F. *Lake Flies and Their Imitation.* Andre Deutsch Ltd, London, 1960.